THE HANDKNITTER'S YARN GUIDE

A visual reference to yarn weights and fibres

Nikki Gabriel

WWW.SEARCHPRESS.COM

A RotoVision Book
Published in 2012 by Search Press Ltd.
Wellwood, North Farm Road,
Tunbridge Wells,
Kent TN2 3DR

This book is produced by
RotoVision
114 Western Rd
Hove
BN3 1DD

ISBN 978-1-84448-750-9

Commissioning Editor: Isheeta Mustafi
Photographers: Simon Punter and Anneliese Hough
Design concept: Emily Portnoi
Artworking: Emma Atkinson
Cover design: Emily Portnoi
Knitting consultant: Tom Van Deijnen
Help with swatches: Gerry Warner

Printing and binding in Singapore by Star Standard Industries (Pte) Ltd.

CONTENTS

USING THIS BOOK

GAUGE AND YARDAGE GUIDES

For every fibre we have included a guide to calculating how much yarn you will need for a specific project, and to help you select a substitute yarn. If you know the weight of the yarn, look for this in the relevant fibre entry, then look along the row to find all the details you will need.

To find the needle size, look at the Recommended Needle Size column for the yarn and ply you are using.

To calculate how many balls of yarn you need, check Yardage per 100g. Let's say you are knitting with a 5-ply silk yarn; the yardage per 100g for 5-ply silk is 270–400yd / 250–360m (see page 59). If you need 300yd / 270m and the yarn is sold in 50g balls, you will need two balls.

If you want to use a yarn other than that specified in a particular pattern, look at the Gauge / Tension column in the guide for your substitute yarn. For it to be a good match, the number of stitches and rows given here will need to be close to those of the yarn given in the pattern.

If you are knitting a jumper or any type of top without a pattern, refer to the appropriate Chest column to find how much yarn you will need.

And if you have a yarn with no label, use the Wraps per Inch column to find the category, gauge and appropriate needle size for it (see page 164).

SWATCHES

In addition to the practical information detailed in the text of this book, the knitted swatches provide a visual guide to how different yarns knit up and to the effects of varying the needle size you select for a particular ply. These swatches give you an idea of the stitch definition to expect from each yarn and of the type of stitch and needle size that best suits them. To allow a direct comparison between stitch types, each swatch has been knitted using the same needle size. Some swatches have been knitted using the recommended needle size for that yarn, some using a larger size, and some a smaller size. The recommended needle size shows the stockinette / stocking stitch swatch at its best. The larger needle size shows the lace stitch at its best. Lace patterns often use a larger needle size than recommended, as this makes the knitted fabric 'lacier'. Where the recommended needle size has been selected, this means that the lace swatch in that set is knitted on a smaller needle size than would generally be used. Many knitters choose to go down a needle size for knitting cables in order to avoid the 'ladder' that is common with cabled knitting, so for some swatches we have chosen a smaller needle size than recommended to show the cable swatch at its best. This makes for a denser fabric and reduces the definition of the stitch in the stockinette / stocking stitch and lace swatches. The 'ladder,' a slight gaping that appears along the left side of the cable, is more noticeable on swatches that have been knitted on the recommended or larger-than-recommended needle size. It is also more noticeable in a static swatch than it would be in a completed garment.

Keep in mind that the most suitable needle size for your desired effect will also depend on your knitting tension. If you are a firm knitter you may need to go up a needle size; if you are a loose knitter, you may need to go down. Remember also that, if you are an uneven knitter, using a larger needle size will magnify any variations in your knitting tension.

We have listed the ply and needle size used below each swatch and highlighted the ply used in the Gauge and Yardage Guide above the swatches. We have also flagged where a needle size has noticeably favoured the knit of one particular stitch, using the key below. With some yarns the effect of a different needle size is more pronounced than with others.

FACTORS AFFECTING STITCH DEFINITION

Variegation
Variegated yarns drown stitch definition. Many knitters choose to use them only for stockinette / stocking stitch.

Fluffiness
Because of their halo, fluffy yarns, such as mohair, angora and eyelash yarns, are not good for stitch definition.

Texture
Boucléd, chenille and slubby yarns (which are unevenly spun), will lead to an unevenness in the knit, and a reduced stitch definition. With eyelash and ladder yarns, the most highly textured yarns available, you will never get any stitch definition.

KEY TO NEEDLE SIZE USED

LARGER
showing lace at its best

SMALLER
showing cable at its best

SUPER FINE, FINE AND LIGHT

Super Fine, Fine and Light yarns are most often used for small pieces because their weight is in proportion with such projects. Popular items are socks, hats, gloves, and baby and children's clothing. These yarns are very economical, as they have more yardage than heavier-weight yarn. The finer-gauge yarns are wonderful for lace designs, and are used to make lightweight shawls, wraps and scarves with complicated and ornate motifs, but they are time-consuming to knit.

2 PLY (LACE / 2 PLY)

The most delicate weight, perfect for knitting babies' items and lace. When lace-weight yarn is knitted, the resulting fabric is usually very thin, with an airy, gossamer texture.

3 PLY (LIGHT FINGERING / 3 PLY)

A slightly heavier choice for baby knits, this is also suitable for all-seasons knits.

4 PLY (FINGERING OR BABY / SOCK OR 4 PLY)

A classic weight for children's knits. The light gauge is the appropriate scale for children's designs and is a great choice for colourful knitting techniques like fair isle or intarsia.

QUICK TIP

Another lightweight yarn is 5 ply (Sport / Light DK or 5 ply). This is a slightly finer version of the versatile DK weight and perfect for bigger lightweight knitting projects including jumpers, blankets and throws. 'Sport' refers to traditional women's ski clothing, such as heirloom jumpers, shawls, wraps and socks.

KNITTING TIPS

- Treat lace yarn gently to avoid breakage and tangling. A yarn swift helps with handling skeins, as it supports without stretching the yarn.

- To avoid visible darning, begin a new skein at the start or end of a row, tie the two ends in a square knot, and thread them in along the garment edge.

- Cast on and bind off loosely to give a neater finish; you can use larger needles for this.

- Fine yarns can be difficult to handle. Wood and bamboo needles are less slippery than aluminium or plastic ones, so can be easier to use with lace yarns, as stitches are less likely to slide off.

2 ply

3 ply

4 ply

MEDIUM

Medium-weight yarns are the most popular knitting yarns; they are extremely versatile, and are comfortable in terms of both warmth and lightness. They are very easy to knit with as they provide great stitch definition and visibility for all levels of knitting skills. Medium-weight yarns are popularly used for jumpers and cardigans, for scarves, hats, and mittens, and for blankets and throws.

8 PLY (LIGHT WORSTED OR DK / DK OR 8 PLY)

8 ply is the most common weight of yarn, and is very versatile. It makes a good fabric for jumpers, wraps, blankets and socks, and is an ideal yarn weight for colourwork and fair-isle knitting. This yarn weight can also be used to make homewares and accessories. It is an easy weight for beginners to learn with, as it has good stitch visibility. This is also a great yarn to use for felting projects, as the resulting fabric is not too heavy.

10 PLY (WORSTED / ARAN OR 10 PLY)

The name of this yarn weight comes from the tradition of knitting thick cable jumpers (sometimes known as Aran or fisherman's jumpers) in Ireland and Scotland; the jumpers get their name from the Aran islands, off the west coast of Ireland. Traditionally, the yarn used for these garments was a natural, raw yarn that created hardy and water-resistant clothing. This weight of yarn is ideal for knitting chunky, warm garments and accessories to keep out the winter chill.

KNITTING TIPS

- Two strands of 4-ply yarn held together can be used instead of a single strand of 8-ply yarn. Similarly, two strands of 8-ply yarn held together can be used instead of a single strand of 10-ply yarn.

- Knitting stitches such as ribbing and cables are highlighted in Medium-weight yarns.

- Medium-weight yarns are easy to handle and work with, as the weight of the yarn feels comfortable in the hand.

- The chunky-patterned stitches knitted in traditional Aran yarns enhance the warmth of a fibre in a garment.

8 ply

10 ply

BULKY AND SUPER BULKY

Bulky yarns are perfect for producing fast knitting projects on big needles. These yarns are thick and warm, and great for quick scarves or beanies, or chunky throws and blankets. Bulky yarns are a good choice for beginner knitters, as they provide the motivation to finish a project without laborious effort. These thick yarns also provide the ultimate fibre experience as they come in a wonderful selection of textures and yarn spins. This yarn weight is also a creative option for the more adventurous knitter who wants to make unique garments, accessories and homewares.

12 PLY (BULKY, RUG OR CRAFT / CHUNKY)

Bulky yarn is ideal for creating fashion-forward garments and a perfect choice where texture is desired. Commonly available as rug yarn, which has a rope-like texture, it facilitates an even knitting tension, as it is easy to handle. These yarns generally have great buoyancy and loft, as a lot of air is captured in between the fibres of a chunky yarn.

14 PLY (SUPER BULKY, ROVING OR POLAR / SUPER CHUNKY OR POLAR)

This is the quickest-knitting of the yarn weights, and perhaps the most fun too. This is a big yarn for big needles; however, these yarns are often not as heavy as you might think, as the yarn spins are quite aerated and super-soft.

Roving, which is a single ply, is usually available in natural fibres and really shows up the fibre, although it can be prone to producing excess fluff. Polar yarns have a tube-like appearance and are often manufactured in synthetic, spongy textures that have good loft. Super Bulky yarns come in a vast array of textured novelty yarns; the choice is wonderful.

KNITTING TIPS

- Knitting with big needles can be hard on your hands. Try using lighter-weight needles in bamboo, or hollow plastic needles, for knitting with Bulky-weight yarns. You could also try using shorter needles to lessen the awkwardness of handling the thick yarn.

- Loosen your tension to get amazing drape from your Bulky-weight yarn, making loose, large stitches. If you are knitting garments, this look can be more flattering for the body than a more firmly knitted bulky fabric.

- For the ultimate Bulky-weight yarn experience, try out unusual and rare artisan and handspun yarns.

- Bulky yarns require less yardage than finer yarns, so you will need less yarn to complete a project.

12 ply

14 ply

WOOL

Wool fibre comes from the fleece of sheep. It is a crimpy and elastic, warm and insulative fibre, and is by far the most popular yarn to knit with. There are several breeds of sheep that provide wool for knitting: the finest quality is merino, while the softest and most expensive is lambswool. Wool is accessibly priced, easy to handle, and has many appealing qualities including drape, resilience and durability. Wool retains air and has superb moisture-resistance and wicking qualities. It also breathes well, making it suitable for both winter and summer knitwear.

Wool is spun in a variety of weights and is often mixed with other fibres to improve its durability and elasticity, and reduce its cost. It is a good choice for babies', children's, and adult's knits, and is available in all weights of yarn from Super Fine to Super Bulky.

SPECS

Source: Sheep fleece

Relative cost: An inexpensive fibre

Range of weights: 1 ply to 14 ply

Range of colours: Naturally coloured wool is creamy white, with varieties of beiges, greys and browns. Wool can be dyed in a vast range of colours, from pastels through to warm, earthy hues and deep, bright colours

USE AND CARE

Washing: Gentle handwash in tepid water, and avoid agitation to avoid shrinkage. Superwash wool can be gently machine-washed. Also dry-cleanable

Drying: Lay flat to dry in the shade

Notes: Do not tumble dry

QUICK TIP

Wool has a strong propensity to felt when untreated; this property can be exploited for fun knitting and craft projects.

GENERAL QUALITIES

Look: Smooth, mid-sheen

Stitch definition: High

Draping: Good-quality wool will have a lovely drape

Pilling: Wool pills naturally, although superwash wool has been chemically treated to reduce this tendvency

Resilience: Good elasticity

Durability: High

Colour retention: Superb

Feel: Fine-quality wool is soft and warm without scratchiness. Lower-grade wool is soft, but can be a little scratchy against the skin

Warmth: Extremely warm yet very light

Breathability: Superb

Moisture resistance: Excellent

Moisture wicking: Excellent

Allergens and toxins: Wool can be allergenic due to dust and mites trapped in its fibres

Fire retardancy: Naturally flame-retardant

Sustainability: Although wool is biodegradable, it is a heavily processed fibre, unless it is organic. Organic wool is produced and harvested without the use of harsh chemicals and pesticides and is an eco-fibre

PROS

✎ Moisture wicking:
Wool has superb moisture-wicking and insulation properties

✎ Warmth:
Wool is a popular choice for warm garments and accessories

✎ Colours:
Wool has superb dye-retention qualities and its handle and lustre improves with colour treatment. Wool comes in a wonderful range of colours

CONS

✎ Pills:
Wool pills naturally due to the constant movement of the microscopic scales in the fibre. The yarn is often chemically treated to overcome this

✎ Allergies:
Although allergies are rare, some people are extremely sensitive to wool and find it scratchy against their skin

BURN TEST

Wool is hard to ignite, but burns with an orange flame and self-extinguishes. It has a burning hair odour.

QUICK FACT

Tweed (of Irish origin) is a slubby, textured, flecked wool yarn that is very warm. Its character is created by the spinning of short, leftover and recycled fibres, which gives it its nubbly appearance. There are many types of fashioned tweeds now available that emulate the appearance of this traditionally spun yarn.

WOOL BLENDS

Wool is a popular fibre to use in yarn blends to improve elasticity, durability, warmth and drape, and to reduce cost. Wool blends are available in a wide range of yarn weights, from Super Fine to Super Bulky, to suit many purposes.

WOOL AND MOHAIR

Wool is blended with mohair to improve mohair's elasticity and even out the furriness of mohair against the skin. This blend is often available in Fine-weight yarns ranging from 2 ply to 5 ply, although heavier weights can be found. These yarns are popular for lace knitting, to create shawls, wraps and scarves, as the wool enhances the drape in this yarn weight. Medium-weight yarn in this blend is a good choice for larger knitting projects such as cardigans and jumpers. Bulky-weight mohair and wool yarns are usually textured and nubbly, and are wonderful for knitting up novelty accessories and fashion projects.

SPECS

Relative cost: A mohair and wool blend is more expensive than a pure wool blend

Range of weights: 2 ply to 14 ply

Range of colours: Muted earthy palettes, pastel hues, vivid and bright shades, and deep jewel colours

USE AND CARE

Washing: Handwash gently and avoid agitation to prevent shrinkage

Drying: Dry flat to avoid warping

Notes: Lightly steam or shake the dry garment to fluff up the surface nap

GENERAL QUALITIES

Look: Light fur halo

Stitch definition: Medium

Draping: The addition of wool improves the drape of this blend

Pilling: This blend can be prone to pilling unless the wool is treated as a superwash fibre

Resilience: The elasticity of the wool maintains shape, compensating for the lack of elasticity in mohair

Durability: Wool adds strength to this fibre blend

Colour retention: Superb

Feel: Feels softer with the addition of wool to mohair

Warmth: The combination of fibres increases warmth

Breathability: Wool improves the breathability of this mix

Moisture resistance: Wool improves the moisture resistance of this blend

Moisture wicking: The addition of wool improves moisture wicking

Allergens and toxins: Both fibres are prone to irritate sensitive skin

Fire retardancy: Low flammability

Sustainability: Mohair is more environmentally friendly than wool, unless the wool is organic

WOOL AND ACRYLIC

Wool is often mixed with acrylic or other synthetic fibres such as nylon polyamide. This mix reduces the price of the yarn and also enhances its durability and colour saturation. Acrylic fibres can also improve the softness of wool against the skin, reducing the harsh scratchiness that wool sometimes has. This is an extremely versatile yarn mix and comes in all plies from 1 ply to 12 ply.

SPECS

Relative cost: A wool and acrylic mix is an economical yarn

Range of weights: 1 ply to 12 ply

Range of colours: Soft and muted pastels to bright and dark colours

USE AND CARE

Washing: Handwash or gentle machine wash

Drying: Dry flat in shade

Notes: Cool iron only

QUICK FACT

Naturally heathered wool yarns are a result of the beautiful colour variations in the fleece of the sheep.

GENERAL QUALITIES

Look: Smooth with mid-sheen

Stitch definition: High

Draping: Good

Pilling: Acrylic yarn reduces the pilling tendency of wool

Resilience: Good elasticity; acrylic reduces the memory of the yarn mix without reducing elasticity

Durability: The addition of acrylic improves the durability of the yarn

Colour retention: Good

Feel: Soft and smooth

Warmth: Temperate warmth against the skin, as acrylic is a cooler fibre than wool

Breathability: Acrylic reduces the breathability of this yarn mix

Moisture resistance: Acrylic reduces moisture resistance in this blend

Moisture wicking: Good

Allergens and toxins: Lower allergy risk with the addition of acrylic

Fire retardancy: Low flammability

Sustainability: Acrylic and wool yarn is not an environmentally friendly yarn mix

WOOL WEIGHTS

FINE WOOL

Fine wool is elastic, strong and soft and is a popular choice for babies' and children's garments. It is also a good choice for delicate, light knits in lacy stitches, or for accessories such as gloves, hats, shawls and scarves. As a fine-gauge yarn, it is smooth and easy to work with. It is usually available in a range of weights from 1 ply to 5 ply.

GAUGE AND YARDAGE GUIDE

WEIGHT	RECOMMENDED NEEDLE SIZE	YARDAGE PER 100G (yd / m)	GAUGE / TENSION (stitches and rows per 4in / 10cm)	CHEST (yd / m) 34–36in / 86–91cm	CHEST (yd / m) 38–40in / 97–101cm	CHEST (yd / m) 42–44in / 107–112cm	CHEST (yd / m) 46–48in / 117–122cm	WRAPS PER INCH
1 ply	0–1 / 2–2.25mm	1,500–1,530 / 1,370–1400	32–34 and 46–48	2,200 / 2,011	2,500 / 2,290	2,800 / 2,560	3,200 / 2,930	35–38
2 ply	2 / 2.75mm	1,000–1,400 / 920–1,280	30–32 and 44–46	2,100 / 1,920	2,400 / 2,190	2,700 / 2,470	3,000 / 2,745	32–35
3 ply	3–4 / 3.25–3.5mm	650–800 / 590–730	28–30 and 42–44	1,900 / 1,740	2,100 / 1,920	2,400 / 2,195	2,700 / 2,470	29–32
4 ply	4–5 / 3.5–3.75mm	440–600 / 400–550	26–28 and 40–42	1,600 / 1,460	2,000 / 1,830	2,300 / 2,100	2,500 / 2,290	27–29
5 ply	5 / 3.75mm	350–500 / 320–450	24–26 and 38–40	1,500 / 1,370	1,800 / 1,650	2,100 / 1,920	2,400 / 2,190	24–27

4-ply 75% polyamide, 25% wool on 2–3 / 3mm needles in stockinette / stocking stitch

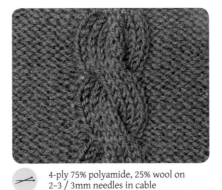

4-ply 75% polyamide, 25% wool on 2–3 / 3mm needles in cable

4-ply 75% polyamide, 25% wool on 2–3 / 3mm needles in lace

MEDIUM WOOL

This is a good yarn weight for jumpers, cardigans, wraps and shawls. It creates warmth without bulk and is great for spectacular colourwork for adults' knits.

GAUGE AND YARDAGE GUIDE

WEIGHT	RECOMMENDED NEEDLE SIZE	YARDAGE PER 100g (yd / m)	GAUGE / TENSION (stitches and rows per 4in / 10cm)	CHEST (yd / m) 34–36in / 86–91cm	CHEST (yd / m) 38–40in / 97–101cm	CHEST (yd / m) 42–44in / 107–112cm	CHEST (yd / m) 46–48in / 117–122cm	WRAPS PER INCH
8 ply	6 / 4mm	230–260 / 210–240	22–24 and 32–34	1,400 / 1,280	1,700 / 1,550	2,000 / 1,830	2,300 / 2,100	20–22
10 ply	8 / 5mm	200–230 / 180–210	18–20 and 30–32	1,300 / 1,190	1,600 / 1,460	1,900 / 1,750	2,200 / 2,010	18–20

10-ply 100% merino wool on 8 / 5mm needles in stockinette / stocking stitch

10 ply 100% merino wool on 8 / 5mm needles in cable

10-ply 100% merino wool on 8 / 5mm needles in lace

BULKY WOOL

This is a soft and warm yarn without too much weight, as wool is airy and lofty. This yarn can be smooth, boucléd or textured and makes great big-knit fashion garments and accessories. This yarn is also useful for homewares such as throws and cushions, and novelty projects such as bags. It also makes wonderful accessories such as hats, shawls, scarves and wraps.

GAUGE AND YARDAGE GUIDE

WEIGHT	RECOMMENDED NEEDLE SIZE	YARDAGE PER 100g (yd / m)	GAUGE / TENSION (stitches and rows per 4in / 10cm)	CHEST (yd / m) 34–36in / 86–91cm	CHEST (yd / m) 38–40in / 97–101cm	CHEST (yd / m) 42–44in / 107–112cm	CHEST (yd / m) 46–48in / 117–122cm	WRAPS PER INCH
12 ply	10$^{1}/_{2}$–13 / 6.5–9mm	100–150 / 90–140	14–16 and 22–26	1,200 / 1,100	1,500 / 1,370	1,800 / 1,650	2,100 / 1,920	14–16
14 ply	15 / 10mm	50–100 / 45–90	12–14 and 16–20	1,100 / 1,005	1,400 / 1,280	1,700 / 1,550	2,000 / 1,830	12–14

12-ply 100% merino wool on 11 / 8mm needles in stockinette / stocking stitch

12-ply 100% merino wool on 11 / 8mm needles in cable

12-ply 100% merino wool on 11 / 8mm needles in lace

MOHAIR

Mohair is a fluffy fibre; the lightest, yet warmest of the animal fibres. Notable for its high lustre and sheen, mohair creates a soft and silky fabric. It is often boucléd or looped, as the mohair fibre has a natural ringlet curl, and is a great textural addition in yarn mixes.

SPECS

Source: Angora goat

Relative cost: A luxury fibre, generally more expensive than wool

Range of weights: 1 ply to 14 ply

Range of colours: Soft pastels and muted earthy tones to bright and rich colours

USE AND CARE

Washing: Can be dry-cleaned or washed on gentle machine cycles

Drying: Lay flat to dry

Notes: To fluff up garment, lightly shake or gently brush down with your hand

GENERAL QUALITIES

Look: Fluffy

Stitch definition: The fluffy nature of mohair makes for low stitch visibility

Draping: Low to medium draping quality, which can be improved by knitting open lace and with bigger needles

Pilling: Long fibres from older goats tend to pill, however, the fine short kid-goat fibres have low pilling

Resilience: High; mohair holds its shape for many wears

Durability: High; strong and extremely durable

Colour retention: Superb

Feel: Although very soft, long mohair fibres can cause itching and irritation to the skin

Warmth: Extremely warm, yet very light

Breathability: A high-loft fibre, mohair breathes well

Moisture resistance: Mohair fabrics are water resistant

Moisture wicking: Fibres carry moisture away from the skin

Allergens and toxins: No harmful allergenic substances; fibres are composed mostly of keratin, a natural protein

Fire retardancy: Naturally flame retardant

Sustainability: Mohair is shorn biannually and provides a sustainable farming enterprise in its own right. Angora goats are usually the preferred species for livestock in fragile landscapes. As long as post-shearing treatments do not involve the use of too many harsh chemical washes, mohair poses a low environmental risk

PROS

Versatility:
An all-seasons fashion fibre, wonderful in warm knits and wovens for cold weather and in airy, lightweight structures that breathe with the body for warm days

Lustre/Sheen:
The fluffy nature of the yarn gives a kind of glow around the fabric

Colour:
Takes dye exceptionally well, which leads to longer-lasting, vibrant colours

Shrink resistance:
Mohair's smooth fibres do not felt and therefore have low shrinkage

Elasticity:
Very elastic – it can be stretched up to 30% and will spring back to shape. Mohair garments resist wrinkling, stretching and sagging

CONS

Sticky:
Because the yarn is so fuzzy and the fibres are clingy, it can be sticky to knit with and is extremely difficult and slow to unpick. A boucléd mohair makes easier knitting

Fluffy:
The long fibres of the mohair can be irritating and cause the skin to itch. The finer kid-mohair fibres are more suitable for garments and a blend with other fibres adds comfort

BURN TEST

A mohair yarn, like most animal fibres, will recoil from flame, smell like burned hair, and turn to ash.

MOHAIR BLENDS

Mohair is an extremely versatile fibre. A lightweight, soft fabric, it is often mixed with other fibres to add these qualities to a yarn. In Light- and Medium-weight yarns, a common mix is with silk, wool and alpaca fibres to add weight for drape and smoothness. For heavier-weight yarns, mohair is a great textural addition in novelty fibre yarns with mixes of acrylic, lurex and polyester.

MOHAIR AND SILK

The addition of silk to mohair lends a smoothness and luxuriousness to its skin-feel. It reduces the irritation caused by the fluff of mohair and enhances the yarn's lustre. It also adds weight, which benefits the draping quality when knitted. This combination makes a very warm and light blend that is perfect for lightweight layering pieces: lace shawls, wraps, scarves and cardigans.

SPECS

Relative cost: A silk blend costs more than pure mohair

Range of weights: 2 ply to 8 ply

Range of colours: Pastels and earthy hues to vivid shades

USE AND CARE

Washing: Handwash in tepid water

Drying: Dry in shade to avoid fading, flat to avoid warping

GENERAL QUALITIES

Look: Light fluff and mid-sheen

Stitch definition: The silk smooths the texture of this yarn, which creates a more visible stitch definition

Draping: Silk improves the draping qualities of mohair as it adds weight to the yarn. The natural elasticity of the mohair maintains shape, compensating for the lack of elasticity in silk

Pilling: Low pilling with the addition of silk

Resilience: Silk has little elasticity so reduces the spring action in this blend

Durability: Excellent; this is a blend of two of the strongest natural fibres

Colour retention: Colour retention in silk is not as strong as mohair—silk can fade in sun, which creates a dappled effect

Feel: Soft; silk adds smoothness to an otherwise hairy yarn

Warmth: Silk increases the warmth of mohair

Breathability: Both are light fibres that breathe readily

Moisture resistance: As silk absorbs moisture, the moisture resistance of mohair is reduced in this blend

Moisture wicking: Good; silk and mohair both draw moisture away from the skin

Allergens and toxins: Silk reduces the tendency of mohair fluff to irritate the skin

Fire retardancy: Good; low flammability

Sustainability: Silk is biodegradable; combined with mohair it is a sustainable blend

MOHAIR AND ACRYLIC

Mohair is often included in Bulky and novelty yarns to add texture and dimension to an acrylic fibre. This creates a strong and durable blend, although rougher against the skin than a soft mohair yarn. The benefit of this type of yarn is its textured and unusual appearance, especially when the mix is with irregular twisted synthetic materials. The acrylic fibre used varies depending on the intended 'look' of the yarn.

SPECS

Relative cost: A mohair–acrylic blend is often inexpensive and sold in large balls that are ideal for a broad range of fun and unusual projects

Range of weights: 2 ply to 14 ply

Range of colours: Soft and muted pastels to bold and mottled, variegated colour combinations

USE AND CARE

Washing: Machine or handwash in cold water

Drying: Do not tumble dry or dry-clean as the synthetic fibres can buckle or melt

Notes: Cool iron only

GENERAL QUALITIES

Look: Fluffy and fleecy

Stitch definition: Low as this yarn combination tends to be hairy or textured

Draping: An acrylic fibre adds durability, elasticity and weight to mohair, improving drape and reducing shrinkage. An acrylic fibre won't stay flat while knitting. Washing care after knitting will improve this

Pilling: High pilling resistance with the addition of acrylic fibre

Resilience: Addition of acrylic improves mohair's resilience as acrylic fibres have high elasticity

Durability: A high-performance yarn with the additional strength from acrylic fibre

Colour retention: A durable, colour-bonding combination. Acrylic fibre, being synthetic, requires a different dye application from a mohair fibre; this is often exploited in designs to give interesting colour variegations

Feel: Scratchier than a pure mohair

Warmth: As acrylic is a cooler fibre than mohair, this combination has reduced warmth

Breathability: Breathes less than a pure mohair

Moisture resistance: Acrylic increases mohair's moisture resistance

Moisture wicking: Superior moisture-wicking properties

Allergens and toxins: Low

Fire retardancy: Good; low flammability

Sustainability: The production of acrylic fibres has high environmental risks, reducing the sustainability of this blend

MOHAIR WEIGHTS

FINE MOHAIR

Fine mohair is perfect for lightweight and lace knitting, and trans-seasonal fashions. Larger needles than what is suggested on the belly band are usually recommended as the fluff of mohair adds extra width to the yarn. It is not an easy yarn to work with, as it can be sticky to unpick and it slides off plastic needles easily; wooden knittiwng needles will make for easier knitting. A bouclé or blended mohair is an easier yarn to manage.

GAUGE AND YARDAGE GUIDE

WEIGHT	RECOMMENDED NEEDLE SIZE	YARDAGE PER 100g (yd / m)	GAUGE / TENSION (stitches and rows per 4in / 10cm)	CHEST (yd / m) 34–36in / 86–91cm	CHEST (yd / m) 38–40in / 97–101cm	CHEST (yd / m) 42–44in / 107–112cm	CHEST (yd / m) 46–48in / 117–122cm	WRAPS PER INCH
1 ply	3–8 / 3.25–5mm	1,000–1,250 / 915–1,140	24–28 and 32	1,300 / 1,190	1,600 / 1,460	1,740 / 1,590	2,200 / 2,010	28
2 ply	3–9 / 3.25–5.5mm	900–920 / 822–842	20–22 and 30	1,100 / 1,005	1,400 / 1,280	1,700 / 1,550	2,000 / 1,830	26
3 ply	3–9 / 3.25–5.5mm	600–870 / 550–800	18–24 and 28	1,090 / 1,000	1,370 / 1,500	1,645 / 1,500	1,920 / 1,760	24
4 ply	8–10 / 5–6mm	400–500 / 360–460	14–18 and 26	1,000 / 915	1,300 / 1,190	1,600 / 1,460	1,900 / 1,740	22

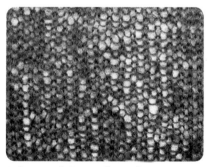

1-ply 70% mohair, 30% silk on 9 / 5.5mm needles in stockinette / stocking stitch

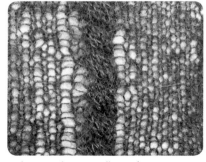

1-ply 70% mohair, 30% silk on 9 / 5.5mm needles in cable

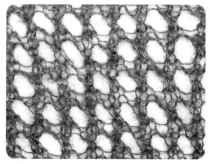

1-ply 70% mohair, 30% silk on 9 / 5.5mm needles in lace

MEDIUM MOHAIR

Medium-weight mohair is often blended with other fibres to improve durability and drape in knitting. Usually the predominant fibre in this weight mix, mohair maintains a lightness and texture in the fabric, but also has some of the qualities of heavier yarns, which makes it good for jumpers, cardigans, wraps and shawls. In the swatches below, the stockinette / stocking stitch and cable swatches would benefit from being knitted on a smaller needle.

GAUGE AND YARDAGE GUIDE

WEIGHT	RECOMMENDED NEEDLE SIZE	YARDAGE PER 100g (yd / m)	GAUGE / TENSION (stitches and rows per 4in / 10cm)	CHEST (yd / m) 34–36in / 86–91cm	CHEST (yd / m) 38–40in / 97–101cm	CHEST (yd / m) 42–44in / 107–112cm	CHEST (yd / m) 46–48in / 117–122cm	WRAPS PER INCH
5 ply	8–10½ / 5–6.5mm	300–380 / 275–350	15–17 and 24	900 / 822	1,200 / 1,100	1,500 / 1,370	1,800 / 1,650	19
8 ply	10–11 / 6–8mm	200–250 / 180–230	14–16 and 22	800 / 730	1,100 / 1,005	1,400 / 1280	1,700 / 1,550	17
10 ply	10½–11 / 6.5–8mm	160–180 / 150–160	12–14 and 20	700 / 640	1,000 / 915	1,300 / 1,190	1,600 / 1,460	15

5-ply 64% kid mohair, 25% wool, 11% nylon on 8 / 5mm needles in stockinette / stocking stitch

5-ply 64% kid mohair, 25% wool, 11% nylon on 8 / 5mm needles in cable

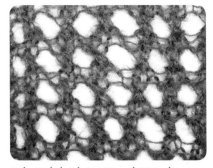

5-ply 64% kid mohair, 25% wool, 11% nylon on 8 / 5mm needles in lace

BULKY MOHAIR

Bulky mohair is usually bouclèd, slubbed or mixed with other fibres for great textural yarns, making it fun for unusual projects. It is perfect for children's projects, blankets and throws, novelty scarves, shawls and wraps, and jackets. Work tightly for a brushed effect, as in the swatch below. The lack of stitch definition is typical of Bulky mohair, and exaggerated by the variegated yarn. As stitch definition is poor with Bulky mohair, we have included only a stockinette / stocking stitch swatch for this yarn.

GAUGE AND YARDAGE GUIDE

WEIGHT	RECOMMENDED NEEDLE SIZE	YARDAGE PER 100g (yd / m)	GAUGE / TENSION (stitches and rows per 4in / 10cm)	CHEST (yd / m) 34–36in / 86–91cm	CHEST (yd / m) 38–40in / 97–101cm	CHEST (yd / m) 42–44in / 107–112cm	CHEST (yd / m) 46–48in / 117–122cm	WRAPS PER INCH
12 ply	10$^{1}/_{2}$–13 / 6.5mm–9mm	140–160 / 130–145	10–12 and 18	600 / 550	900 / 820	1,200 / 1,100	1,500 / 1,370	12–14
14 ply	10–15 / 6–10mm	180–200 / 165–180	8–14 and 16	500 / 460	800 / 730	1,100 / 1,005	1,400 / 1,280	22–24

12-ply 72% mohair, 16% wool, 12% polyester on 10 / 6mm needles in stockinette / stocking stitch

ANGORA

Angora fibre comes from the fur of the angora rabbit. It is one of the finest of the natural fibres, and is fluffy, light, soft and very warm. Knitted up, its nap creates a cloud-like appearance with a silky feel. Used for its fibres as early as the mid-18th century for French royalty, angora is still considered a 'noble fibre' and is an expensive luxury yarn, as it takes a lot of hands-on care to tend to the rabbits and maintain their prized coats. Angora is a very fine and short fibre that is commonly spun in yarn weights from 4 ply to 8 ply. To produce heavier plies such as 10 ply and 12 ply, angora is generally mixed with other fibres.

SPECS

Source: The coat of the angora rabbit

Relative cost: An expensive fibre

Range of weights: 2 ply to 12 ply

Range of colours: Naturally coloured angora comes in a range of around ten colours, from white to black, with greys and beiges in between. Dyed angora yarn is available in a range of pastels and brights

USE AND CARE

Washing: Can be dry-cleaned or handwashed with cold water

Drying: Lay flat to dry

Notes: To fluff up an angora garment, lightly shake it or gently brush down with the hand

GENERAL QUALITIES

Look: Fluffy

Stitch definition: The fluffy nature of angora makes for low stitch visibility

Draping: Has low draping qualities, which can be improved by working open lace or using larger needles

Pilling: Has a tendency to pill, although the pills are easily picked off by hand

Resilience: Angora is an inelastic fibre and is prone to warping unless mixed with another fibre

Durability: A strong and extremely durable fibre

Colour retention: Superb

Feel: Soft and silky

Warmth: Extremely warm yet very light

Breathability: Angora is a high-loft fibre and breathes well

Moisture resistance: Angora fabrics are naturally water-resistant

Moisture wicking: One of the best moisture-wicking fibres of all the animal fibres

Allergens and toxins: No harmful allergenic substances, as the fibres are composed mostly of keratin, a natural protein; however, the short, fluffy fibres can irritate the nose

Fire retardancy: Angora fabrics are naturally flame-resistant

Sustainability: The farming of angora rabbits is a sustainable practice, and as these are usually small-scale enterprises, do not consume a lot of energy. The fibres are 'plucked' seasonally as the rabbits naturally shed their coats, and the animals are not harmed in the shearing process

PROS

- ✎ Softness:
  Angora is an extremely soft and silky fibre
- ✎ Warmth:
  One of the warmest yet lightest of the natural fibres, as it has high insulation properties
- ✎ Natural colours:
  A beautiful range of natural tones is available, from pure white through to greys and blacks, warm beiges and browns
- ✎ Non-odour-absorbing:
  Angora is naturally resistant to odours

CONS

- ✎ Slippery:
  Angora can be very slippery to knit with; wooden needles might be the best option to counter this
- ✎ Fluffy:
  The short fibres of angora garments can come loose and irritate a wearer's nose. Angora fibres can also shed excessively
- ✎ Lack of stain resistance:
  Angora is less stain-resistant than most natural fibres

BURN TEST

Angora burns briefly and self-extinguishes. It smells like burning hair or feathers.

ANGORA BLENDS

Angora is an inelastic fibre and is often mixed with other fibres such as wool and/or nylon to improve this. Because of angora's fluffy character, small quantities may be added to blends to create a 'halo' on the yarn's surface. Mixed angora fibres make beautiful jumpers and socks.

QUICK TIPS

Only wash an angora garment when soiled; too much cleaning can break down the yarn.

Angora is seven times warmer than wool. In extremely cold and snowy climates, angora can be used to make thermal underwear.

ANGORA AND WOOL

The addition of wool to angora creates a more elastic and resilient yarn that is also less expensive. The wool adds just enough drape to the fabric to be beneficial, while the presence of the angora maintains a lightness and loft in the blend. Wool reduces the irritation of the fluff of angora, while angora adds softness to the yarn blend. Often a tweedy wool yarn is mixed with angora to add luxury and softness to this otherwise scratchy fibre. This fibre combination is usually available in 5-ply and 8-ply yarns, and sometimes in a chunky 12-ply weight. It is a very warm blend that is lovely to use for cardigans, jumpers and accessories.

SPECS

Relative cost: An angora and wool blend is less expensive than a pure angora blend

Range of weights: 5 ply and 8 ply are popular weights; 12 ply is sometimes available

Range of colours: Pastel hues to vivid shades

USE AND CARE

Washing: Handwash in cold water

Drying: Dry flat to avoid warping

Notes: Lightly steam or shake the dry garment to fluff up the surface nap

GENERAL QUALITIES

Look: Light fluff, light nubbly texture, low sheen

Stitch definition: The wool smooths the texture of the angora yarn and thereby improves stitch definition

Draping: Wool improves the draping qualities of angora as it adds a little weight to the yarn mix

Pilling: Unless a superwash wool is used, this blend can be prone to some pilling

Resilience: The natural elasticity of wool maintains shape, compensating for the lack of elasticity in the angora

Durability: A good, strong fibre blend

Colour retention: Good

Feel: Angora adds softness, while wool adds smoothness to the blend

Warmth: Increased warmth

Breathability: Increased breathability as angora has high loft, while wool already has wonderful breathable qualities

Moisture resistance: Both fibres offer excellent moisture-resistance

Moisture wicking: Both fibres have good moisture-wicking properties

Allergens and toxins: Angora is hypoallergenic, while wool reduces the irritation of fluff for sensitive skin

Fire retardancy: Low flammability

Sustainability: Angora is biodegradable and a clean fibre, which somewhat reduces the the environmental impact of the blend, as wool fibre requires heavy processing

ANGORA, COTTON AND ACRYLIC/NYLON

Angora is often included in a blend to add a slight halo of fluff and warmth to an otherwise smooth and cool fibre such as cotton. Additionally, an acrylic or nylon fibre may be added to improve the elasticity, creating an all-purpose and all-season yarn blend.

SPECS

Relative cost: An angora, cotton and acrylic blend is less expensive than a pure angora blend

Range of weights: 4 ply to 5 ply

Range of colours: Soft and muted pastels

USE AND CARE

Washing: Handwash or gently machine wash in cold water

Drying: Do not tumble dry or dry-clean, as the synthetic fibres can buckle or melt

Notes: Cool iron only

GENERAL QUALITIES

Look: Slightly fluffy and matte texture; slightly mottled coloration

Stitch definition: Good

Draping: Good draping quality from the cotton and nylon/acrylic

Pilling: Brushed cotton combined with angora can cause low pilling

Resilience: Nylon improves the elasticity in this yarn blend

Durability: Cotton and nylon improve the overall performance of this yarn blend

Colour retention: Excellent

Feel: Soft

Warmth: Angora adds some warmth and counters the coolness of the other fibres in the blend, creating a good temperature-balanced yarn

Breathability: Angora and cotton have excellent breathability qualities; if nylon, which lacks this quality, is used in a small quantity in the blend, the yarn will still retain good breathability

Moisture resistance: Low moisture resistance, as cotton tends to absorb moisture

Moisture wicking: Good moisture-wicking properties

Allergens and toxins: Low allergy risk

Fire retardancy: Cotton is more flammable than angora and nylon, which is likely to make up the largest percentage of this yarn blend

Sustainability: The addition of cotton and nylon to this blend reduces the environmental friendliness of this yarn blend

ANGORA WEIGHTS

FINE ANGORA

Angora is soft and warm as a Fine yarn and is usually spun in a 4- or 5-ply weight. It is an inelastic yarn, but as a pure fibre blend it is good for knitting lace and open-work stitches. It has a low stitch definition, but creates a fine cloud-like halo when knitted up. In a yarn blend, it is good for baby knits and socks.

GAUGE AND YARDAGE GUIDE

WEIGHT	RECOMMENDED NEEDLE SIZE	YARDAGE PER 100g (yd / m)	GAUGE / TENSION (stitches and rows per 4in / 10cm)	CHEST (yd / m) 34–36in / 86–91cm	CHEST (yd / m) 38–40in / 97–101cm	CHEST (yd / m) 42–44in / 107–112cm	CHEST (yd / m) 46–48in / 117–122cm	WRAPS PER INCH
2 ply	1–2 / 2.25–2.75mm	800–900 / 730–820	36–38 and 50–52	1,800 / 1,650	2,300 / 2,100	2,600 / 2,380	2,900 / 2,650	23–25
4–5 ply	1–3 / 2.25–3.25mm	700–800 / 640–730	28–34 and 46–48	1,700 / 1,550	2,100 / 1,920	2,500 / 2,290	2,700 / 2,470	21–23

2-ply 100% angora on 0 / 2mm needles in stockinette / stocking stitch

2-ply 100% angora on 0 / 2mm needles in cable

2-ply 100% angora on 0 / 2mm needles in lace

MEDIUM ANGORA

Medium-weight angora is a popular yarn weight. It is a very furry yarn and looks great when knitted up as mittens, scarves or hats. It is an extremely soft yarn, but it is inelastic. It can be difficult to work with and slippery on the needles, although using wooden knitting needles can alleviate this. Angora fibre blended with elastic and smooth fibres such as wool makes knitting easier.

GAUGE AND YARDAGE GUIDE

WEIGHT	RECOMMENDED NEEDLE SIZE	YARDAGE PER 100g (yd / m)	GAUGE / TENSION (stitches and rows per 4in / 10cm)	CHEST (yd / m) 34–36in / 86–91cm	CHEST (yd / m) 38–40in / 97–101cm	CHEST (yd / m) 42–44in / 107–112cm	CHEST (yd / m) 46–48in / 117–122cm	WRAPS PER INCH
8 ply	0–2 / 2–2.75mm	500–600 / 460–550	26–28 and 36–40	1,600 / 1,465	2,000 / 1,830	2,400 / 2,190	2,700 / 2,470	17–19
10 ply	8 / 5mm	300–400 / 275–365	22–24 and 32–34	1,500 / 1,370	1,900 / 1,740	2,300 / 2,100	2,600 / 2,380	13–15

8-ply 100% angora on 4 / 3.5mm needles in stockinette / stocking stitch

8-ply 100% angora on 4 / 3.5mm needles in cable

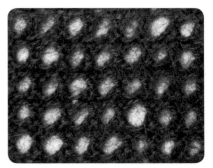

8-ply 100% angora on 4 / 3.5mm needles in lace

BULKY ANGORA

Angora usually forms a small percentage in a blend with other fibres in Bulky-weight yarns; it adds luxury and loft to the mix. Textured wool such as tweed will benefit from the extra softness of angora in a mix. The airiness of angora lightens a knobbly, bulky yarn blend both visually and structurally. It is a great choice for making warm garments and accessories.

GAUGE AND YARDAGE GUIDE

WEIGHT	RECOMMENDED NEEDLE SIZE	YARDAGE PER 100g (yd / m)	GAUGE / TENSION (stitches and rows per 4in / 10cm)	CHEST (yd / m) 34–36in / 86–91cm	CHEST (yd / m) 38–40in / 97–101cm	CHEST (yd / m) 42–44in / 107–112cm	CHEST (yd / m) 46–48in / 117–122cm	WRAPS PER INCH
12 ply	10½ / 6.5mm	100–200 / 91–185	18–20 and 24–26	1,600 / 1,460	2,000 / 1,830	2,400 / 2,200	2,600 / 2,380	9–11

12-ply 100% angora on 11 / 8mm needles in stockinette / stocking stitch

12-ply 100% angora on 11 / 8mm needles in cable

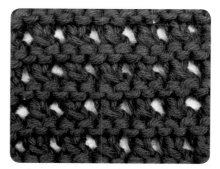

12-ply 100% angora on 11 / 8mm needles in lace

CASHMERE

Cashmere fibre derives from the coat of the Kashmir goat and its subspecies. Cashmere is an expensive, highly prized and luxurious fibre; its high status and expense are due to its scarce supply as well as the superb quality of the yarn. Cashmere is a fine, light, warm fibre with a soft halo. The finest cashmere fibres are short, and these are separated from the longer, coarser fibres of the goat's molted coat in a time-consuming process called 'dehairing'.

Cashmere is usually available in Fine- and Medium-weight yarns. Knitted up, it creates a warm, insulative fabric without bulk that makes beautiful jumpers, cardigans and accessories. It is often blended with other fibres to provide a luxury yarn at a more accessible price. As a blend it comes in all weights including Bulky. Cashmere is a good choice for heirloom knits that will be treasured forever.

SPECS

Source: The coat of the Kashmir goat

Relative cost: An expensive fibre

Range of weights: 4 ply to 8 ply; 10 ply to 12 ply in blends

Range of colours: Naturally coloured cashmere comes in white, although rarely; it is more common in browns and greys. Dyed cashmere is available in a range of pastels, warm earthy tones and deep and bright hues

QUICK FACT

It takes one goat four years to yield enough fibre to make one jumper.

USE AND CARE

Washing: Dry-clean or gentle handwash

Drying: Lay flat to dry

Notes: Avoid agitation during washing, as shrinkage will occur

GENERAL QUALITIES

Look: Fuzzy

Stitch definition: Low stitch definition due to its fuzzy surface

Draping: Good-quality cashmere will have a soft drape

Pilling: Has a tendency to pill, but frequent washing will reduce this

Resilience: Low elasticity

Durability: The short staple fibres are susceptible to early weakening

Colour retention: Superb

Feel: Soft and smooth

Warmth: Extremely warm yet very light

Breathability: The fibres are so fine that they do not breathe as well as other natural fibres; knitting with more open stitches or lace stitches improves this

Moisture resistance: Excellent

Moisture wicking: Good

Allergens and toxins: Cashmere allergies are less common than wool allergies, but the symptoms are similar. This is due to fungi and dust trapped in the fibres

Fire retardancy: Naturally flame-retardant

Sustainability: The Kashmir goat is indigenous to mountainous and/or desert climates and thrives in these environments. Cashmere is a low environmental hazard if the goats are farmed in this habitat

PROS

↗ Softness:
Extremely soft and silky; the softness improves with wearing

↗ Warmth:
Provides warmth and insulation without bulk

↗ Natural colours:
A beautiful range of natural tones is available, from pure whites and greys to blacks, warm beiges and browns

CONS

↗ Poor durability:
Weakens with wear

↗ Pilling:
Cashmere's short staple fibres make it susceptible to pilling

BURN TEST

Cashmere burns with an orange flame and self-extinguishes. It has a burning hair odour and leaves dark ashy powder when crushed

CASHMERE BLENDS

Cashmere is often mixed with other fibres to add a touch of luxury to cheaper yarn blends. Usually only a small amount of cashmere is needed to add a halo, softness, warmth and loft to a yarn. These blends are sumptuous and feel lovely on the skin while being much less expensive than pure cashmere. Cashmere blends make lovely accessories such as gloves, hats, scarves, shawls and socks. They also make wonderful jumpers and cardigans and knitted fashion items such as skirts and legwarmers.

CASHMERE AND SILK

For a truly luxurious yarn blend, cashmere and silk make great partners. Silk adds strength and high lustre and enhances the softness of cashmere against the skin. Both fibres are light yet warm, and are good for inter-season knitting. This is an inelastic fibre blend, and is more suitable to fine, lacy knits as it is usually spun as a lightweight yarn.

SPECS

Relative cost: A silk and cashmere yarn blend is an expensive yarn

Range of weights: 2 ply to 5 ply

Range of colours: From soft, muted pastels to bright and dark colours

USE AND CARE

Washing: Handwash

Drying: Dry flat in shade

Notes: Cool iron only

GENERAL QUALITIES

Look: Brushed with high sheen

Stitch definition: Medium stitch definition, improved by the addition of silk

Draping: Medium draping quality

Pilling: Low pilling

Resilience: Low elasticity

Durability: Improved durability with the addition of silk

Colour retention: Silk will fade in sunlight and become dappled over time unless dried in the shade

Feel: Soft and smooth

Warmth: Temperate warmth against the skin

Breathability: Average, unless knitted as lacy openwork

Moisture resistance: High moisture resistance with the addition of silk

Moisture wicking: Improved moisture wicking with the addition of silk

Allergens and toxins: Low allergy risk as silk is hypoallergenic

Fire retardancy: Low flammability

Sustainability: A low environmental risk

CASHMERE AND WOOL

This is a popular yarn blend, as wool has greater durability and elasticity than cashmere and makes a practical yarn mix. It also provides a lower-cost yarn that retains some of the luxurious softness and lightness that cashmere endows. Mixed with the weight and springiness of wool, there is just enough extra drape and resilience to create a perfect fabric. It is spun in a variety of yarn weights from Fine to Bulky, and is very versatile.

SPECS

Relative cost: A cashmere and wool blend is less expensive than a pure cashmere

Range of weights: 2 ply to 12 ply

Range of colours: From muted, earthy palettes and pastel hues to vivid, bright shades and deep jewel colours

USE AND CARE

Washing: Handwash gently and avoid agitation to prevent shrinkage

Drying: Dry flat to avoid warping

Notes: Dry-cleanable

GENERAL QUALITIES

Look: Smooth, subtle halo, high lustre

Stitch definition: High stitch definition

Draping: Lovely draping quality from the softness of cashmere and some weight from the wool

Pilling: Can be prone to pilling unless the wool is treated as a superwash fibre

Resilience: The natural elasticity of wool maintains shape, compensating for the lack of elasticity in cashmere

Durability: Wool adds strength to this fibre blend

Colour retention: Superb

Feel: Soft and velvety

Warmth: Increased warmth from the cashmere

Breathability: Increased breathability from the wool

Moisture resistance: Both fibres have excellent moisture-resistance properties

Moisture wicking: Both fibres have good moisture-wicking properties

Allergens and toxins: Both fibres are prone to trigger allergic responses

Fire retardancy: Low flammability

Sustainability: Wool is a heavily processed fibre, and although cashmere is mostly processed by hand and is less of an environmental risk, its percentage in this blend is usually small. Consequently, this is a less sustainable yarn blend than a pure cashmere yarn

CASHMERE WEIGHTS

FINE CASHMERE

Cashmere is desirable as a finely spun yarn as it has a lofty, soft essence yet is still very warm. It is like a second skin to wear as a jersey knit, while as an open-lace knit it breathes well in temperate climates. Fine-weight cashmere is spun in weights from 2 ply to 5 ply. It is often knitted up to make small and treasurable accessories, but is also used for bigger projects such as heirloom shawls or special-occasion jumpers.

GAUGE AND YARDAGE GUIDE

WEIGHT	RECOMMENDED NEEDLE SIZE	YARDAGE PER 100g (yd / m)	GAUGE / TENSION (stitches and rows per 4in / 10cm)	CHEST (yd / m) 34–36in / 86–91cm	CHEST (yd / m) 38–40in / 97–101cm	CHEST (yd / m) 42–44in / 107–112cm	CHEST (yd / m) 46–48in / 117–122cm	WRAPS PER INCH
2 ply	2 / 2.75mm	1,000–1,020 / 915–930	32–34 and 46–48	2,100 / 1,920	2,500 / 2,290	2,800 / 2,560	3,200 / 2,930	23–24
3 ply	3–4 / 3.25–3.5mm	900–1,000 / 820–915	28–30 and 38–40	1,800 / 1,650	2,200 / 2,010	2,600 / 2,380	2,800 / 2,560	21–22
4 ply	4–5 / 3.5–3.75mm	650–800 / 600–730	26–28 and 34–36	1,700 / 1,550	2,100 / 1,920	2,500 / 2,290	2,700 / 2,470	19–20
5 ply	5–6 / 3.75–4mm	320–500 / 290–460	22–24 and 26–30	1,600 / 1,460	2,000 / 1,830	2,400 / 2,190	2,600 / 2,380	16–18

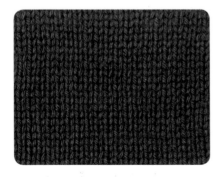

4-ply 100% cashmere on 4 / 3.5mm needles in stockinette / stocking stitch

4-ply 100% cashmere on 4 / 3.5mm needles in cable

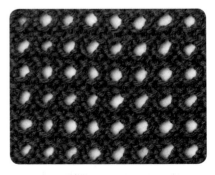

4-ply 100% cashmere on 4 / 3.5mm needles in lace

MEDIUM CASHMERE

This is a good yarn weight for jumpers, cardigans, wraps and shawls. It provides warmth without the bulk of a warm-weight yarn, and it is often mixed to create a less expensive luxury yarn.

GAUGE AND YARDAGE GUIDE

WEIGHT	RECOMMENDED NEEDLE SIZE	YARDAGE PER 100g (yd / m)	GAUGE / TENSION (stitches and rows per 4in / 10cm)	CHEST (yd / m) 34–36in / 86–91cm	CHEST (yd / m) 38–40in / 97–101cm	CHEST (yd / m) 42–44in / 107–112cm	CHEST (yd / m) 46–48in / 117–122cm	WRAPS PER INCH
8 ply	6 / 4mm	200–250 / 180–230	20–22 and 24–26	1,400 / 1,280	1,600 / 1,460	1,900 / 1,740	2,100 / 1,920	14–15
10 ply	8 / 5mm	180–196 / 165–180	18–20 and 20–22	1,300 / 1,190	1,500 / 1,370	1,700 / 1,550	1,900 / 1,740	12–13

8-ply 100% cashmere on 6 / 4mm needles in stockinette / stocking stitch

8-ply 100% cashmere on 6 / 4mm needles in cable

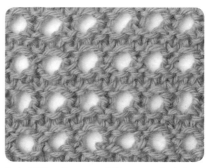

8-ply 100% cashmere on 6 / 4mm needles in lace

BULKY CASHMERE

Soft and warm without the heaviness or over-drape of a chunky yarn, this is often a mixed yarn weight, usually with wool or cotton. Using a smaller needle would help to reduce the ladder effect in the cable swatch.

GAUGE AND YARDAGE GUIDE

WEIGHT	RECOMMENDED NEEDLE SIZE	YARDAGE PER 100g (yd / m)	GAUGE / TENSION (stitches and rows per 4in / 10cm)	CHEST (yd / m) 34–36in / 86–91cm	CHEST (yd / m) 38–40in / 97–101cm	CHEST (yd / m) 42–44in / 107–112cm	CHEST (yd / m) 46–48in / 117–122cm	WRAPS PER INCH
12 ply	10½–13 / 6.5–9mm	80–120 / 75–110	12–14 and 16–18	800 / 730	1,000 / 915	1,200 / 1,095	1,500 / 1,370	9–11

12-ply 100% cashmere on 10 / 6mm needles in stockinette / stocking stitch

12-ply 100% cashmere on 10 / 6mm needles in cable

12-ply 100% cashmere on 10 / 6mm needles in lace

CAMEL

Camel fibre comes from the fleece of the Bactrian (two-humped) camel. A rare and exotic yarn, camel's soft, downy fibre has characteristics that are very similar to cashmere. However, it is less expensive than cashmere, and the demand for it is not so high. Its short, hollow fibre makes it airy, lightweight, soft, and warm, with wonderful insulating properties. The molting camel fibre is plucked and dehaired to separate the shorter, finer fibres from the longer, coarser ones. These short fibres are used for knitting yarns, with the baby camel fibres being particularly prized.

Camel is usually spun as 5-ply, 8-ply, or 10-ply weights, with Fine and Bulky yarn spins available in blends, offered in a range from 2 ply to 12 ply. Camel is also available as artisan handspun yarns, which are generally soft and sometimes slubby with a fine halo. These are great for socks, hats and scarves, and for larger items such as jumpers and cardigans. Because of their rugged, good-looking, natural shades, they are a popular choice for men's knits. Camel is often mixed with wool to improve strength and reduce cost.

SPECS

Source: The coat of the Bactrian camel

Relative cost: An expensive fibre

Range of weights: 5 ply to 12 ply

Range of colours: The natural camel colour is red-brown; dyed shades are dark and muted. While white and light camel shades are available, they are much scarcer and more expensive

USE AND CARE

Washing: Handwash in lukewarm water with mild detergent

Drying: Lay flat to dry

Notes: Can be dry-cleaned with perchlorethylene or fluorocarbon

GENERAL QUALITIES

Look: Light halo with soft sheen

Stitch definition: Good

Draping: Wonderful drape

Pilling: Does not pill

Resilience: Low elasticity

Durability: The short fibres have low strength

Colour retention: Superb

Feel: Soft and smooth

Warmth: Extremely warm yet very light

Breathability: Excellent

Moisture resistance: Excellent

Moisture wicking: Good moisture-wicking properties

Allergens and toxins: Non-allergenic

Fire retardancy: Naturally flame-retardant

Sustainability: The camel thrives in nomadic desert environments and camel-yarn production is a sustainable farming practice

PROS

- **Softness:**
  Extremely soft; the softness improves with wearing
- **Warmth:**
  Offers warmth and insulation without bulk
- **Anti-pilling:**
  Does not pill
- **Dyed shades:**
  Dyes up in beautiful deep and muted tones
- **Anti-static:**
  Removes static stress

CONS

- **Fragile:**
  Like cashmere, camel's short fibres are prone to early weakening

QUICK TIP

The warmth and natural lanolin from camel fibre has therapeutic healing effects for the skin.

BURN TEST

Camel burns with an orange flame and self-extinguishes. It has a burning hair odour and leaves a dark ash powder when crushed.

CAMEL BLENDS

Camel is often mixed with wool or with silk to improve its durability. The soft halo and coloration of the camel adds a rustic depth and charm to these fibre blends.

CAMEL AND SILK

Silk adds strength, lustre and drape to this yarn blend. It is a sumptuous mix and dyes up beautifully. It is lovely knitted in lacy and open-work stitches to make shawls and scarves that cascade off the body. This is a lightweight yet warm yarn blend, and is often spun as a 5 ply. It is good for temperate winter climates or in-between seasons.

SPECS

Relative cost: A silk and camel yarn blend is expensive

Range of weights: 2 ply to 5 ply

Range of colours: Soft and muted pastels to bright and dark colours

USE AND CARE

Washing: Handwash

Drying: Dry flat in shade

Notes: Cool iron only

GENERAL QUALITIES

Look: High lustre with a soft halo; sometimes slubby

Stitch definition: Good

Draping: Superb draping quality

Pilling: No pilling

Resilience: Low elasticity

Durability: Improved durability with the addition of silk

Colour retention: Silk will fade in sunlight and become dappled over time unless dried in the shade

Feel: Soft and silky

Warmth: Temperate warmth against the skin

Breathability: Good

Moisture resistance: High

Moisture wicking: Good

Allergens and toxins: No allergy risk

Fire retardancy: Low flammability

Sustainability: A low environmental risk

QUICK TIP

Camel yarn is excellent for socks as the fibre is moisture-absorbing and breathable.

CAMEL WEIGHTS

FINE CAMEL

Fine camel has all the characteristics of cashmere in its softness, warmth and lofty luxurious texture. However, it is not as popular, and is still relatively underrated, particularly as a Fine-weight yarn. Although it is usually labelled as a Fine weight, on closer inspection, fine camel yarns are often slightly heavier than standard. Fine camel is usually found in 2-ply to 5-ply yarn and variations of these weights in between. Fine camel makes beautiful socks, baby clothes and accessories, and is especially good for showcasing fine lace knitting.

GAUGE AND YARDAGE GUIDE

WEIGHT	RECOMMENDED NEEDLE SIZE	YARDAGE PER 100g (yd / m)	GAUGE / TENSION (stitches and rows per 4in / 10cm)	CHEST (yd / m) 34–36in / 86–91cm	CHEST (yd / m) 38–40in / 97–101cm	CHEST (yd / m) 42–44in / 107–112cm	CHEST (yd / m) 46–48in / 117–122cm	WRAPS PER INCH
2–3 ply	2–3 / 2.75–3.25mm	730 / 670	28 and 33–35	1,500 / 1,370	1,900 / 1,740	2,200 / 2,010	2,500 / 2,290	22–24
4–5 ply	4–5 / 3.5–3.75mm	370 / 340	24–26 and 30–32	1,200 / 1,100	1,500 / 1,370	1,800 / 1,645	2,100 / 1,920	18–20

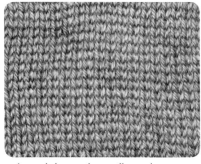

4-ply 35% baby camel, 65% silk on 5 / 3.75mm needles in stockinette / stocking stitch

4-ply 35% baby camel, 65% silk on 5 / 3.75mm needles in cable

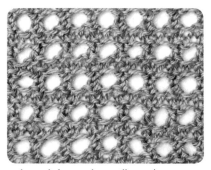

4-ply 35% baby camel, 65% silk on 5 / 3.75mm needles in lace

MEDIUM CAMEL

Camel is more popular as a Medium-weight yarn. This is because it tends to be marketed as a rare, exotic fibre, suited to a more rustic, provincial and artisanal use. All these characteristics are perfect for knitting jumpers and homewares such as cushions and throws. This weight is also suitable for accessories, such as scarves, mittens and hats, and for garments such as delicate cardigans and jumpers, as it is a temperate yarn against the skin. It is usually available in 8-ply and 10-ply yarn weights.

GAUGE AND YARDAGE GUIDE

WEIGHT	RECOMMENDED NEEDLE SIZE	YARDAGE PER 100g (yd / m)	GAUGE / TENSION (stitches and rows per 4in / 10cm)	CHEST (yd / m) 34-36in / 86-91cm	CHEST (yd / m) 38-40in / 97-101cm	CHEST (yd / m) 42-44in / 107-112cm	CHEST (yd / m) 46-48in / 117-122cm	WRAPS PER INCH
8 ply	6-7 / 4-4.5mm	200-250 / 180-230	19-22 and 27-29	1,100 / 1,005	1,400 / 1,280	1,700 / 1,550	1,900 / 1,740	15-17
10 ply	8-9 / 5-5.5mm	190-200 / 170-180	18-20 and 23-25	1,000 / 915	1,300 / 1,190	1,500 / 1,370	1,800 / 1,650	13-14

10-ply 85% extra-fine merino, 15% camel on 6 / 4mm needles in stockinette / stocking stitch

10-ply 85% extra-fine merino, 15% camel on 6 / 4mm needles in cable

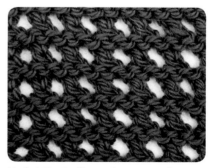

10-ply 85% extra-fine merino, 15% camel on 6 / 4mm needles in lace

BULKY CAMEL

Soft and warm without the heaviness or over-drape of a chunky yarn, this weight of camel yarn is usually available as a blend, most often with wool. This yarn weight is good for chunky accessories such as scarves and hats, or for men's jumpers and cardigans. Although generally good for stitch definition, the heathered colouring and slight fluffiness of the yarn obscures the definition in the swatches below.

GAUGE AND YARDAGE GUIDE

WEIGHT	RECOMMENDED NEEDLE SIZE	YARDAGE PER 100g (yd / m)	GAUGE / TENSION (stitches and rows per 4in / 10cm)	CHEST (yd / m) 34–36in / 86–91cm	CHEST (yd / m) 38–40in / 97–101cm	CHEST (yd / m) 42–44in / 107–112cm	CHEST (yd / m) 46–48in / 117–122cm	WRAPS PER INCH
12 ply	10¹/₂–13 / 6.5–9mm	90–100 / 85–90	12–14 and 21–22	800 / 730	1,000 / 915	1,200 / 1,100	1,500 / 1,370	11–12

12-ply 100% handspun camel on 10¹/₂ / 6.5mm needles in stockinette / stocking stitch

12-ply 100% handspun camel on 10¹/₂ / 6.5mm needles in cable

12-ply 100% handspun camel on 10¹/₂ / 6.5mm needles in lace

ALPACA

Alpaca fibre comes from the fleece of the alpaca, a domesticated species of South American camelid. This is a herd animal that looks like a small llama. There are two types of alpaca fibres: the more common Huacya, which produces a dense, soft, crimpy fibre; and the rarer Suri, which has a mop of silky pencil-like locks resembling dreadlocks.

Alpaca is a dense fibre that is fine, soft and smooth. It is also very warm; it has unique thermal properties due to the microscopic air pockets found in the fibre. Alpaca is spun in a variety of yarn weights from 1 ply to 14 ply. The fibres contain no lanolin, and alpaca is therefore hypoallergenic, making it suitable for baby knits and knits for people with sensitive skin. Alpaca is wonderful to use for all knitting projects, and is often mixed with other fibres to improve its over-drape, durability and cohesion. It comes in an amazing variety of natural colours, from pure black to white, with warm greys and browns in between.

SPECS

Source: The fleece of the Huacya or Suri alpaca

Relative cost: An expensive fibre

Range of weights: 1 ply to 14 ply

Range of colours: Naturally coloured alpaca comes in pure white to blue-black and up to 28 shades of greys, browns, and beiges. Dyed alpaca is available in a range of pastels, warm, earthy tones, and deep and bright hues

USE AND CARE

Washing: Dry-clean or gentle handwash

Drying: Lay flat to dry to avoid sagging

Notes: Lightly steam or lightly shake to fluff up surface nap

GENERAL QUALITIES

Look: Smooth with light brush and high lustre

Stitch definition: Good

Draping: Strong draping qualities

Pilling: Does not pill but does tend to shed lightly

Resilience: High elasticity

Durability: Fibres are susceptible to weakening

Colour retention: Superb

Feel: Smooth and silky

Warmth: Extremely warm and dense

Breathability: Breathes well

Moisture resistance: Excellent

Moisture wicking: Good

Allergens and toxins: Hypoallergenic

Fire retardancy: Naturally flame-retardant

Sustainability: Alpaca farming has a low environmental impact

PROS

- **Softness:**
  Extremely soft and silky
- **Warmth:**
  Has superb warmth and insulating properties
- **Natural colours:**
  A beautiful range of natural tones is available, from pure whites and greys to blacks, warm beiges and browns

CONS

- **Over-drape:**
  Excessive 'give' can create over-drape in knitting. To prevent over-drape in your knitting, work to a tighter tension by using smaller needles than recommended

BURN TEST

Alpaca, like most animal hair fibre, burns with an orange flame and self-extinguishes. It has the odour of burning hair and leaves a dark ash powder when crushed.

ALPACA BLENDS

Alpaca is often found in yarn blends, and is prized for the smoothness and warmth it adds to a mix. Alpaca blends are available in a wide variety of yarn weights from 1 ply to 14 ply.

ALPACA AND WOOL

A popular choice as wool has good resilience, which improves the tension in this blend. Alpaca also adds smoothness and alleviates the scratchiness of wool against the skin. This yarn mix is available in Fine weights from 2 ply to 5 ply. It is often used for accessories such as socks, gloves, hats and scarves. This blend is also popular as an 8-ply weight for knitting high-fashion garments. The rarer, yet exciting blends are the 10-ply and 12-ply yarns that make fabulous chunky accessories and garments that benefit from drape.

SPECS

Relative cost: An alpaca and wool blend is less expensive than a pure alpaca yarn

Range of weights: 1 ply to 14 ply

Range of colours: From muted earthy palettes and pastel hues to vivid and bright shades and deep jewel colours

USE AND CARE

Washing: Handwash gently

Drying: Dry flat to avoid warping

Notes: Dry-cleanable

GENERAL QUALITIES

Look: Smooth, subtle brush and high lustre

Stitch definition: High stitch definition

Draping: Alpaca's tendency to over-drape is countered by the resilience of the wool

Pilling: Can be prone to pilling unless the wool is treated as a superwash fibre

Resilience: The natural elasticity of the wool maintains shape, compensating for the over-drop of alpaca

Durability: Wool adds strength to this fibre

Colour retention: Superb

Feel: Soft and velvety

Warmth: Wool regulates the very warm alpaca

Breathability: Improved by the wool

Moisture resistance: Good: both fibres have excellent moisture-resistance

Moisture wicking: Good: both fibres have good moisture-wicking properties

Allergens and toxins: Alpaca reduces the allergic risk in this blend

Fire retardancy: Low flammability

Sustainability: Wool is a heavily processed fibre, and although alpaca has a more sustainable farming practice, the addition of wool makes this a less sustainable yarn blend overall

ALPACA AND SILK

Two luxurious soft fibres against the skin make this a beautiful yarn blend. Silk is a light and inelastic fibre, so benefits from the addition of the weight and drape of alpaca. Both fibres are extremely warm, so are usually spun in Fine weights, from 2 ply to 5 ply. These yarns are ideal for making warm garments without bulk with open-work or fine lacy stitches.

SPECS

Relative cost: A silk and alpaca yarn blend is expensive

Range of weights: 2 ply to 5 ply

Range of colours: Soft and muted pastels to bright and dark colours

USE AND CARE

Washing: Handwash

Drying: Dry flat in shade

Notes: Cool iron only

GENERAL QUALITIES

Look: Brushed with high sheen

Stitch definition: Good

Draping: Good

Pilling: Low pilling

Resilience: Medium elasticity

Durability: Improved durability with the addition of silk

Colour retention: Silk will fade in sunlight and become dappled over time unless dried in the shade

Feel: Soft, silky and smooth

Warmth: Warm against the skin

Breathability: Average, unless knitted as lacy or open-work fabric

Moisture resistance: High

Moisture wicking: Good

Allergens and toxins: Low allergy risk

Fire retardancy: Low flammability

Sustainability: A low environmental risk

ALPACA WEIGHTS

FINE ALPACA

Alpaca as a Fine weight is a favourable yarn choice, as its natural warmth and density are rare advantages in a lightweight yarn.
It is beautiful to use for baby knits, lace knitting and accessories, such as shawls and wraps, that will benefit from the lovely drape.

GAUGE AND YARDAGE GUIDE

WEIGHT	RECOMMENDED NEEDLE SIZE	YARDAGE PER 100g (yd / m)	GAUGE / TENSION (stitches and rows per 4in / 10cm)	CHEST (yd / m) 34–36in / 86–91cm	CHEST (yd / m) 38–40in / 97–101cm	CHEST (yd / m) 42–44in / 107–112cm	CHEST (yd / m) 46–48in / 117–122cm	WRAPS PER INCH
1 ply	2 / 2.75mm	920–1,000 / 840–915	32–34 and 49–51	2,000 / 1,830	2,300 / 2,105	2,600 / 2,380	2,900 / 2,650	42–44
2 ply	2 / 2.75–3mm	822–870 / 750–795	30–32 and 46–48	1,900 / 1,740	2,100 / 1,920	2,400 / 2,195	2,700 / 2,470	39–41
3 ply	3–4 / 3.25–3.5mm	550–700 / 502–640	26–28 and 43–45	1,700 / 1,550	2,000 / 1,830	2,300 / 2,105	2,600 / 2,380	35–37
4 ply	4–5 / 3.5–3.75mm	430–600 / 390–550	22–24 and 40–42	1,500 / 1,370	1,800 / 1,650	2,100 / 1,920	2,400 / 2,190	30–33
5 ply	6–8 / 4–5mm	220–320 / 200–290	20–22 and 34–38	1,400 / 1,280	1,700 / 1,550	2,000 / 1,830	2,300 / 2,100	24–28

2-ply 75% alpaca, 20% silk, 5% cashmere on 2 / 2.75mm needles in stockinette / stocking stitch

2-ply 75% alpaca, 20% silk, 5% cashmere on 2 / 2.75mm needles in cable

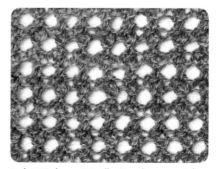

2-ply 75% alpaca, 20% silk, 5% cashmere on 2 / 2.75mm needles in lace

MEDIUM ALPACA

This is a weighty and luxuriously soft and warm yarn weight to knit with. It is good for creating garments that benefit from drape, as this yarn weight has a strong tendency to drop. Alpaca is often blended with more resilient yarns to improve its stitch memory and springiness.

GAUGE AND YARDAGE GUIDE

WEIGHT	RECOMMENDED NEEDLE SIZE	YARDAGE PER 100g (yd / m)	GAUGE / TENSION (stitches and rows per 4in / 10cm)	CHEST (yd / m) 34–36in / 86–91cm	CHEST (yd / m) 38–40in / 97–101cm	CHEST (yd / m) 42–44in / 107–112cm	CHEST (yd / m) 46–48in / 117–122cm	WRAPS PER INCH
8 ply	6–8 / 4–5mm	250–280 / 230–256	18–24 and 26–30	1,300 / 1,190	1,600 / 1,460	1,900 / 1,740	2,100 / 1,920	17–20
10 ply	8 / 5mm	250–300 / 230–275	18–20 and 23–25	1,200 / 1,100	1,500 / 1,370	1,700 / 1,550	1,900 / 1,740	13–16

8-ply 100% alpaca on 6 / 4mm needles in stockinette / stocking stitch

8-ply 100% alpaca on 6 / 4mm needles in cable

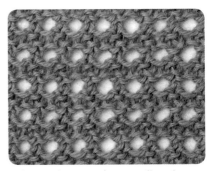

8-ply 100% alpaca on 6 / 4mm needles in lace

BULKY ALPACA

Alpaca is usually found in blends at this weight; it is usually mixed with strong, resilient fibres to create more buoyant yarn. As a pure yarn blend, it is still an interesting yarn to work with, as it has a wonderful soapy-smooth texture and is very warm. It is good for fashion knitting for items such as bags, and chunky hats and scarves.

GAUGE AND YARDAGE GUIDE

WEIGHT	RECOMMENDED NEEDLE SIZE	YARDAGE PER 100g (yd / m)	GAUGE / TENSION (stitches and rows per 4in / 10cm)	CHEST (yd / m) 34–36in / 86–91cm	CHEST (yd / m) 38–40in / 97–101cm	CHEST (yd / m) 42–44in / 107–112cm	CHEST (yd / m) 46–48in / 117–122cm	WRAPS PER INCH
12 ply	10½–13 / 6.5–9mm	80–120 / 75–110	12–14 and 20–22	900 / 820	1,100 / 1,000	1,300 / 1,190	1,600 / 1,460	11–12
14 ply	15 / 10mm	50–70 / 45–65	8–10 and 16–18	800 / 730	1,000 / 915	1,200 / 1,100	1,500 / 1,370	9–10

14 ply 100% alpaca on 15 / 10mm needles in stockinette / stocking stitch

14-ply 100% alpaca on 15 / 10mm needles in cable

14-ply 100% alpaca on 15 / 10mm needles in lace

SILK

Silk is unwound from the fibres of the cocoon of the *Bombyx mori* moth—the mulberry silkworm. Three types of silk come from this species. The finest quality is reeled silk, which is spun directly from the cocoon into a shiny, smooth and pure-white yarn. The raw material left behind from this process is carded and processed into spun silk, which is a lustrous, creamy-coloured yarn. The short waste fibres from this stage are spun into noil silk yarn, which is low-sheen, textured, nubbly and an oat-white colour. Spun silk is most commonly used for knitting yarns; it has high lustre, luxurious softness, and lightness with a heavenly drape.

Silk is mostly spun as a Fine-weight yarn, from 1 ply to 3 ply. Because it is expensive, the fine plies are considered better value because of their generous yardage. These yarns make beautiful fine-knit garments, heirloom pieces and baby knits. Less common (because of their high price) are Medium-weight silky yarns, which will transform an ordinary knitting pattern into an extraordinary item. Silk is also spun into heavier-weight yarns, in both mixed and pure blends. These are wonderful to use for lace knitting and for chunky accessories. The yarn spins and plies affect the handle of silk. Spun tightly and plied higher, it is stronger but less yielding and stiffer in appearance. Spun loosely and plied less, it is softer with a higher sheen, although the thread tends to be slightly weaker.

SPECS

Source: The cocoon of the *Bombyx mori* moth

Relative cost: An expensive fibre

Range of weights: 1 ply to 12 ply

Range of colours: Naturally coloured silk comes in a range from pure whites through to cream and gold honey tones. When dyed, it comes in a range of colours from pastels to bright jewel tones and rich, dark colours

USE AND CARE

Washing: Dry-clean or gentle handwash

Drying: Dry flat in the shade otherwise the colour will fade

Notes: Cool iron

GENERAL QUALITIES

Look: Spun silk: smooth and shiny; noil: textured and nubbly

Stitch definition: Spun silk: high stitch definition; noil: medium stitch definition

Draping: Lovely drape

Pilling: Reeled silk does not pill; noil is a short fibre and has a greater tendency to pill, although gassing (burning off of excess fluff) reduces this

Resilience: Low elasticity

Durability: Reeled silk and tightly plied spun silks are very strong; noil silk fibres in low-twist yarns tend to be weaker

Colour retention: Superb dye absorption, although colour fades in sunlight

Feel: Soft and smooth

Warmth: Excellent insulation properties; retains warmth in cold weather and coolness in hot weather

Breathability: Excellent

Moisture resistance: High moisture resistance; stays dry, resisting mildew and mould absorption

Moisture wicking: Good

Allergens and toxins: A low allergenic fibre

Fire retardancy: High flammability, with higher burning rate than other fibres

Sustainability: Silk is biodegradable. However, the production of reeled silk in particular is an ethical and fair-trade issue, as it involves destroying many moths for their cocoons and relies on cheap labour. Some spun silks, silk noils, and wild silks fall under the banner of 'peace' or 'vegetarian' silks; these are spun from cocoons without killing the moths and their production is managed by ethical cooperatives

PROS

✍ **Softness:**
Extremely soft and lustrous against the skin

✍ **Insulative:**
Warm in cool weather; cool in warm weather

CONS

✍ **Catchy:**
Can tend to catch easily, although more tightly plied and twisted yarns are less prone to this

✍ **Static:**
Silk is susceptible to static cling

BURN TEST

Silk has the odour of burning hair and burns readily, but not necessarily with a steady flame. When the flame is extinguished it turns to ash.

QUICK FACT

Wild silk (also known as tussah or Assam silk) is harvested in Asia from silk moths that resist domestication. There are many types of wild silk, produced in golden amber and honey colours. These are slightly coarser than mulberry-silk yarn, but still lustrous, with interesting and unique textures.

QUICK TIP

Silk odours, caused by alkaline amines, can be neutralised by soaking the fibre or garment in a bucket of water to which a small amount of citric acid, such as vinegar, or pH-balanced detergent or shampoo, has been added.

SILK BLENDS

Silk is often mixed with other fibres to add luxury to yarn blends. The addition of silk usually softens a yarn and improves its drape, lustre, insulation and loft. The whole range of yarn weights is spun in silk blends and the variety of fibre blends is large, suiting many different purposes. Spun silk fibre adds smoothness and lustre to a yarn, while noil fibres add texture and character. The addition of silk usually increases the price of a yarn blend, so you may want to reserve such yarns for special projects.

QUICK TIP

Silk is slippery to work with and is often supplied in skeins that require winding into balls. Use a yarn winder for your skein, placing it on the side to give easier movement. To prevent a tangled mess in the ball, try winding the yarn around a cardboard tube, such as a toilet-paper roll. This needs to be done tightly by hand.

SILK AND WOOL

This is a popular yarn blend, as wool greatly improves the elasticity and lowers the price of the yarn mix. Silk adds smoothness to the blend, and reduces the scratchiness that wool tends to have against the skin. If a noil yarn is used, it creates a textured, nubbly appearance. This blend benefits from the extra strength of the wool fibre. It is spun in many weights, from Fine to Bulky, and has many applications, from accessories to garments and homewares.

SPECS

Relative cost: A silk and wool blend is less expensive than a pure silk blend

Range of weights: 2 ply to 12 ply

Range of colours: From muted, earthy palettes in light and dark shades to pastel hues and bright colours

USE AND CARE

Washing: Handwash gently; dry-cleanable

Drying: Dry flat to avoid warping

Notes: Dry in shade to avoid colour fading

GENERAL QUALITIES

Look: Wool mixed with spun silk: smooth, high sheen; wool mixed with noil silk: matte, nubbly

Stitch definition: Good stitch definition

Draping: Lovely draping quality from the softness of silk and the addition of some weight from the wool

Pilling: Can be prone to pilling unless the wool and/or silk is treated

Resilience: The elasticity of the wool maintains shape, compensating for the lack of elasticity in silk

Durability: Wool adds strength to this fibre blend

Colour retention: Superb colour application, although silk can fade in sunlight, creating a dappled effect

Feel: Soft and velvety

Warmth: Increased warmth from the silk

Breathability: Both fibres have good breathability

Moisture resistance: Both fibres have excellent moisture-resistance properties

Moisture wicking: Both fibres contribute good moisture-wicking properties

Allergens and toxins: Silk is a low allergenic fibre, but wool can trigger allergic responses

Fire retardancy: Low flammability

Sustainability: Wool is a heavily processed fibre, and silk is considered unethical in its manufacture. This blend is not considered a sustainable fibre unless the wool is organic and the silk is 'peace' or 'vegetarian' silk

SILK AND BAMBOO

Silk, being so light, is often mixed with cool fibres such as cotton, linen and bamboo to add lustre, drape and extra insulation and luxury to those summery yarn blends. The addition of bamboo in a silk yarn makes a lightweight, cool, soft and smooth yarn mix. Silk adds a lovely shiny finish and drape and reduces the splitting tendency of bamboo in a yarn blend. Bamboo improves the hypoallergenic quality and wrinkle-resistance in this yarn. This blend is great for baby knits in a 2- or 3-ply yarn. It is also wonderful to use as a Medium-weight yarn for summer knits. This blend will maintain coolness against the skin and provide ultraviolet protection, as this is a property of bamboo.

SPECS

Relative cost: A silk and bamboo yarn blend is expensive

Range of weights: 2 ply to 8 ply

Range of colours: Soft, muted pastels to bright and dark colours

USE AND CARE

Washing: Handwash

Drying: Dry flat in shade

Notes: Cool iron only

GENERAL QUALITIES

Look: Smooth, high twist, high lustre

Stitch definition: Good

Draping: Good

Pilling: Low pilling

Resilience: Low elasticity

Durability: Good strength in both fibres

Colour retention: Silk will fade in sunlight and become dappled over time

Feel: Soft, smooth and cool

Warmth: Temperate and good for in-between seasons, as silk is insulative, retaining warmth in cold weather and coolness in hot weather

Breathability: Both fibres have good breathability

Moisture resistance: High

Moisture wicking: Good

Allergens and toxins: Low allergy risk

Fire retardancy: Low flammability

Sustainability: A low environmental risk, as both silk and bamboo are biodegradable

SILK WEIGHTS

FINE SILK

Fine silk yarn is a pleasure to knit with, as it is so smooth and lustrous. Because of its fineness, it is best suited to smaller items such as accessories and baby knits. However, the temptation of a more glamorous knit may beckon, as this shiny fibre will transform an ordinary article into something wondrous. Fine silk is often blended with other fibres to suit different temperatures and fashions.

GAUGE AND YARDAGE GUIDE

WEIGHT	RECOMMENDED NEEDLE SIZE	YARDAGE PER 100g (yd / m)	GAUGE / TENSION (stitches and rows per 4in / 10cm)	CHEST (yd / m) 34–36in / 86–91cm	CHEST (yd / m) 38–40in / 97–101cm	CHEST (yd / m) 42–44in / 107–112cm	CHEST (yd / m) 46–48in / 117–122cm	WRAPS PER INCH
1 ply	1 / 2.25mm	900–1,000 / 825–915	32–34 and 43–44	2,000 / 1,830	2,300 / 2,100	2,500 / 2,290	2,800 / 2,560	30–33
2 ply	2 / 2.75mm	800–900 / 730–822	30–32 and 41–42	1,900 / 1,740	2,100 / 1,920	2,400 / 2,190	2,700 / 2,470	27–29
3 ply	3–4 / 3.25–3.5mm	600–800 / 550–730	28–30 and 38–40	1,800 / 1,650	2,000 / 1,830	2,300 / 2,100	2,600 / 2,380	25–26
4 ply	4–5 / 3.5–3.75mm	500–700 / 450–640	26–28 and 35–37	1,700 / 1,550	1,900 / 1,740	2,100 / 1,920	2,500 / 2,290	23–24
5 ply	5 / 3.75mm	270–400 / 250–360	20–24 and 32–34	1,600 / 1,460	1,800 / 1,650	2,000 / 1,830	2,400 / 2,190	21–22

2-ply 100% silk on 2 / 2.75mm needles in stockinette / stocking stitch

2-ply 100% silk on 2 / 2.75mm needles in cable

2-ply 100% silk on 2 / 2.75mm needles in lace

MEDIUM SILK

This is a good yarn weight for jumpers, cardigans, wraps and shawls. It is warm without the bulk of a warm-weight yarn, and is often mixed with other fibres to create a less expensive luxury yarn. The yarn used in the swatches below has natural flecks and strands of varying width, which will always give an uneven appearance to your knitting.

GAUGE AND YARDAGE GUIDE

WEIGHT	RECOMMENDED NEEDLE SIZE	YARDAGE PER 100g (yd / m)	GAUGE / TENSION (stitches and rows per 4in / 10cm)	CHEST (yd / m) 34–36in / 86–91cm	CHEST (yd / m) 38–40in / 97–101cm	CHEST (yd / m) 42–44in / 107–112cm	CHEST (yd / m) 46–48in / 117–122cm	WRAPS PER INCH
8 ply	6 / 4mm	200–250 / 180–230	14–18 and 29–30	1,500 / 1,370	1,700 / 1,560	1,900 / 1,740	2,300 / 2,100	19–20
10 ply	8 / 5mm	185–190 / 170–175	18–20 and 26–28	1,400 / 1,280	1,600 / 1,465	1,800 / 1,650	2,200 / 2,010	17–19

8-ply 40% lambswool, 25% silk, 25% nylon, 10% kid mohair on 6 / 4mm needles in stockinette / stocking stitch

8-ply 40% lambswool, 25% silk, 25% nylon, 10% kid mohair on 6 / 4mm needles in cable

8-ply 40% lambswool, 25% silk, 25% nylon, 10% kid mohair on 6 / 4mm needles in lace

BULKY SILK

Soft and warm without the heaviness or over-drape of a chunky yarn, this is often a mixed yarn weight, usually blended with wool, cotton, alpaca and mohair. It is often available as a handspun artisan yarn, in an array of unique colorations and textures. It is a great yarn to use for novelty scarves and mittens, and fashion jumpers.

GAUGE AND YARDAGE GUIDE

WEIGHT	RECOMMENDED NEEDLE SIZE	YARDAGE PER 100g (yd / m)	GAUGE / TENSION (stitches and rows per 4in / 10cm)	CHEST (yd / m) 34–36in / 86–91cm	CHEST (yd / m) 38–40in / 97–101cm	CHEST (yd / m) 42–44in / 107–112cm	CHEST (yd / m) 46–48in / 117–122cm	WRAPS PER INCH
12 ply	10½–13 / 6.5–9mm	80–160 / 75–145	12–14 and 19–20	1,200 / 1,100	1,500 / 1,370	1,700 / 1,560	2,000 / 1,830	15–16

12-ply 50% merino, 50% silk on 11 / 8mm needles in stockinette / stocking stitch

12-ply 50% merino, 50% silk on 11 / 8mm needles in cable

12-ply 50% merino, 50% silk on 11 / 8mm needles in lace

COTTON

Cotton, a natural cellulose fibre, makes an inelastic yarn. It is spun either as a combed cotton, which is brushed, matte, and low-twist; or as a mercerised cotton, which is treated to give it a shiny finish and a high twist. Both are durable yarns and soft to work with. The finest-grade cottons are referred to as pima and Egyptian.

SPECS

Source: The cotton plant

Relative cost: An inexpensive fibre

Range of weights: 3 ply to 14 ply

Range of colours: Natural hues and soft pastels to brilliant brights

USE AND CARE

Washing: Can be washed and dried on regular machine cycles

Drying: Lay flat to dry to avoid stretching a garment out of shape

Notes: Dark colours tend to bleed. Adding vinegar to washes alleviates some colour running

GENERAL QUALITIES

Look: combed cotton: smooth and matte; mercerised cotton: smooth and shiny

Stitch definition: High

Draping: Good

Pilling: Fine cotton has high pilling resistance; some brushed cottons are prone to pilling

Resilience: Cotton's lack of elasticity means that knits are prone to stretching and sagging

Durability: Hard-wearing with high tensile strength, so easy to wash

Colour retention: Mercerised cotton has superb colour retention; with brushed cotton all colours tend to fade, and dark colours tend to bleed

Feel: Cool against the skin

Warmth: Low

Breathability: High

Moisture resistance: Low

Moisture wicking: Cotton absorbs moisture readily, which makes a light, breathable fabric in warm weather

Allergens and toxins: Hypoallergenic

Fire retardancy: Poor; cotton is highly flammable

Sustainability: Unless it is organic, cotton cultivation involves the use of many pesticides. Organically grown cotton is a steadily developing trend in farming; it produces equally strong and durable yarn

BURN TEST

Cotton is a plant fibre. When ignited, it burns with a steady flame and smells like burning leaves. The ash loft behind crumbles easily.

PROS

- **Smoothness:**
  Cotton is an extremely smooth fibre with very good stitch definition. It is great for showing off fancy stitch work
- **Draping:**
  Cotton makes a dense and soft fabric when knitted, and has a wonderful drape
- **Lustre/Sheen:**
  Mercerised cotton has a high lustre and is spun in many threads, giving a lovely depth to the fabric
- **Colour range:**
  Cotton yarn is available in a dizzying array of colours

CONS

- **Sagging:**
  Cotton has no spring, so items knitted in pure cotton can sag under their own weight. Cotton is often blended with other fibres to improve this tendency. Machine drying can also correct a saggy garment
- **Sleek:**
  Cotton shows up every aspect of knitting, so any mistakes may be clearly visible
- **Twist:**
  Some cottons, in particular mercerised cottons, have high twist properties and can therefore knit on an angle
- **Splitting:**
  Cotton yarn is prone to splitting during knitting
- **Flammable:**
  Cotton is the most flammable of all natural and synthetic fibres

COTTON BLENDS

Although very soft and drapey, cotton, being inelastic, is quite a rigid yarn to knit with. It is often blended with more resilient fibres, such as wool and nylon, to improve its bounce and elasticity, or with firm fibres, such as linen and silk, to improve its traction.

COTTON AND WOOL

Wool adds just enough elasticity to inflexible cotton, while cotton adds a softer handle to wool. This blend gives a light yarn that is perfect for between-seasons knitting. Usually spun in 4-ply and 8-ply weights, this blend makes wonderful children's knits, hats, socks, jumpers, cardigans, wraps and shawls. This blend usually takes on a heathered look as the two fibres absorb dye differently.

SPECS

Relative cost: Usually less expensive than a pure wool blend

Range of weights: 4 ply to 8 ply

Range of colours: Muted tones

USE AND CARE

Washing: Handwash

Drying: Dry flat

Notes: Wash colours separately

GENERAL QUALITIES

Look: Slightly mottled

Stitch definition: High

Draping: This blend benefits from the natural draping qualities of cotton, but will resist excessive sagging with the resilience of the wool

Pilling: Residual fluff from both fibres may cause this yarn to pill over time

Resilience: Improved elasticity with the addition of wool

Durability: This makes a highly durable blend

Colour retention: Some fading will occur in the cotton, whereas the wool will hold its colour. A garment will take on an aged look after a few washes, which may or may not be desired

Feel: The addition of cotton softens the abrasiveness of wool

Warmth: This blend is cooler than a pure wool blend

Breathability: Improved with the addition of cotton

Moisture resistance: Improved with the addition of wool

Moisture wicking: High

Allergens and toxins: The addition of cotton lowers allergenic reactions to wool

Fire retardancy: Wool is naturally fire-retardant and reduces the flammability of cotton

Sustainability: Cotton is less sustainable than wool; unless both the cotton and the wool are organic, this blend has a low sustainability rating

COTTON WEIGHTS

FINE COTTON

Fine cotton will create soft, light and airy summer knits with drape. Its hypoallergenic qualities make it a good choice for babies' and children's knits. Cotton is an inflexible yarn and can make for tough knitting. It is often blended with more elastic fibres to improve its resilience. To achieve a firm tension and avoid sagging, it may help to use a smaller needle size than recommended.

GAUGE AND YARDAGE GUIDE

WEIGHT	RECOMMENDED NEEDLE SIZE	YARDAGE PER 100g (yd / m)	GAUGE / TENSION (stitches and rows per 4in / 10cm)	CHEST (yd / m) 34–36in / 86–91cm	CHEST (yd / m) 38–40in / 97–101cm	CHEST (yd / m) 42–44in / 107–112cm	CHEST (yd / m) 46–48in / 117–122cm	WRAPS PER INCH
3–4 ply	2–3 / 2.75–3.25mm	400–436 / 365–400	28–30 and 39–41	1,600 / 1,460	1,900 / 1,740	2,200 / 2,010	2,500 / 2,290	22–24
5 ply	4–5 / 3.5–3.75mm	300–350 / 275–320	25–27 and 36–38	1,500 / 1,370	1,800 / 1,650	2,100 / 1,920	2,400 / 2,195	20–22

4-ply 100% mercerised cotton on 2–3 / 3mm needles in stockinette / stocking stitch

4-ply 100% mercerised cotton on 2–3 / 3mm needles in cable

4-ply 100% mercerised cotton on 2–3 / 3mm needles in lace

MEDIUM COTTON

A medium-weight cotton creates well-defined stitches. It is usually not recommended for beginners, as it shows up irregular tension. Although heavy in weight, cotton is cool and breathes against the skin, so it is perfect for trans-seasonal fashions. Cotton yarns blended with elastic fibres are easier to handle, and are great for knitting socks. In the swatches below, the stockinette / stocking stitch and cable swatches would benefit from being knitted on a smaller needle.

GAUGE AND YARDAGE GUIDE

WEIGHT	RECOMMENDED NEEDLE SIZE	YARDAGE PER 100g (yd / m)	GAUGE / TENSION (stitches and rows per 4in / 10cm)	CHEST (yd / m) 34–36in / 86–91cm	CHEST (yd / m) 38–40in / 97–101cm	CHEST (yd / m) 42–44in / 107–112cm	CHEST (yd / m) 46–48in / 117–122cm	WRAPS PER INCH
8 ply	4–6 / 3.5–4mm	300–330 / 275–300	20–24 and 28–32	1,450 / 1,325	1,750 / 1,600	2,150 / 1,965	2,450 / 2,240	18–19
10 ply	7 / 4.5mm	190–220 / 175–200	16–18 and 24–26	1,300 / 1,190	1,600 / 1,460	1,900 / 1,740	2,200 / 2,010	14–16

8-ply 100% pima cotton on 7 / 4.5mm needles in stockinette / stocking stitch

8-ply 100% pima cotton on 7 / 4.5mm needles in cable

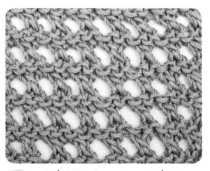

8-ply 100% pima cotton on 7 / 4.5mm needles in lace

BULKY COTTON

Cotton can be very heavy in Bulky-weight yarn, so is usually designed as a blend, novelty or tape yarn to create a more airy structure. If it is handspun, it is generally low-twist to keep it as light as possible. This yarn weight is great for chunky knits without excessive warmth. It is best to keep the work loose, as there is little elasticity, although snags are a disadvantage.

GAUGE AND YARDAGE GUIDE

WEIGHT	RECOMMENDED NEEDLE SIZE	YARDAGE PER 100g (yd / m)	GAUGE / TENSION (stitches and rows per 4in / 10cm)	CHEST (yd / m) 34–36in / 86–91cm	CHEST (yd / m) 38–40in / 97–101cm	CHEST (yd / m) 42–44in / 107–112cm	CHEST (yd / m) 46–48in / 117–122cm	WRAPS PER INCH
12 ply	10–11 / 6–8mm	100–120 / 90–110	12–14 and 20–22	1,200 / 1,095	1,500 / 1,370	1,800 / 1,650	2,100 / 1,920	10–12
14 ply	11–15 / 8–10mm	60–80 / 55–75	8–12 and 16–18	1,000 / 915	1,300 / 1,190	1,500 / 1,370	1,800 / 1,650	8–9

12-ply 100% organic cotton on 10¹/₂–11 / 7mm needles in stockinette / stocking stitch

12-ply 100% organic cotton on 10¹/₂–11 / 7mm needles in cable

12-ply 100% organic cotton on 10¹/₂–11 / 7mm needles in lace

LINEN

Linen is a cellulose fibre that comes from the flax plant. It is an elegant fibre, and the strongest of the vegetable fibres. It is inelastic and wrinkles easily, which is part of its charm. Linen is cool, fresh and soft against the skin, and improves with washing and age. The finest-grade fibres are smooth with a high lustre. Linen's bloom is more evident when it is less bleached and less coloured. Fine linen is a good choice of yarn for lace knitting in accessories such as wraps, scarves and shawls, or for cool summer jumpers and cardigans in Medium-weight yarns.

SPECS

Source: Flax plant

Relative cost: An expensive fibre as it goes through a labour-intensive production process

Range of weights: 4 ply to 12 ply

Range of colours: Natural colours ranging from creamy beiges to light bluey-greys; dyed in colours ranging from soft pastels and muted tones to brights and deep earthy colours

USE AND CARE

Washing: Can be washed on regular machine cycles

Drying: Can be dried on regular machine cycles

Notes: Hot iron

GENERAL QUALITIES

Look: Thick and thin—high-quality fibres are smooth with high natural lustre; lower-grade fibres are wrinkly and slubby

Stitch definition: Good

Draping: Linen has no elasticity so drapes under its own weight, but does not sag as it has a good memory

Pilling: Linen is resistant to pilling

Resilience: Good

Durability: Hard-wearing with high tensile strength, so easy to wash

Colour retention: Absorbs dye less readily than cotton, but has a natural lustre, which benefits from coloration

Feel: Cool, soft and leathery against the skin

Warmth: Low

Breathability: Breathes well and conducts heat away from the body, making it a perfect summer yarn

Moisture resistance: Low

Moisture wicking: Linen absorbs moisture readily, which makes it a light, breathable fabric in warm weather

Allergens and toxins: Linen is a cellulose fibre and is considered hypoallergenic

Fire retardancy: Linen is as highly flammable as cotton

Sustainability: Unless it is organic, linen cultivation involves the use of many pesticides, and linen production uses many chemicals that pollute waterways. Organically grown linen is a gradually developing trend, and it produces equally strong and durable yarn

PROS

🪡 **Lightweight:**
Linen is crisp, flowing and lightweight, making it perfect for warm-weather knits

🪡 **Easy-care:**
Linen is machine-washable and its softness improves over time

🪡 **Durability:**
Because of the length of its fibres, linen makes a strong knitted fabric

🪡 **Hypoallergenic:**
Linen is antistatic and mould-resistant due to the breathability of the fibre

CONS

🪡 **Creasing:**
Linen has no spring due to its inelasticity and creases easily. If creased regularly in the same fold, the fibres will weaken in that area

🪡 **Splitting:**
Linen is prone to splitting during knitting if it is spun as a low-twist yarn

BURN TEST

Linen takes longer to ignite than cotton and is easily extinguished by blowing on it as you would a candle.

QUICK FACT

Wet spinning is a technique used for finer linen to create cohesion in the yarn. This yarn is usually a 1 ply. A dry-spun linen yarn is much coarser.

QUICK TIPS

Always test your swatch by machine-washing and drying it before measuring, as the linen changes during this treatment.

Linen yarn is slippery to knit with; using wooden knitting needles might make handling easier.

LINEN BLENDS

Linen is an expensive fibre and is often blended with other fibres to lower its price. A most common blend is with rayon, as the fibres complement each other for lightweight, cool functionality. Blends that create a warmer fibre suitable for making inter-season garments might include alpaca or wool.

LINEN AND RAYON

Rayon imitates the feel and texture of linen, but it is a cheaper fibre, lowering the price of this yarn blend. Rayon also absorbs dye readily, improving the lustre and colour retention in this mix. It is a strong and durable fibre blend. It is suitable for lightweight summer garments and is usually spun in 5-ply or 8-ply weights. As a Medium-weight yarn, it is available in 10-ply yarn.

SPECS

Relative cost: Less expensive than a pure linen

Range of weights: 5 ply to 10 ply

Range of colours: Natural, muted and pastel tones to dark, earthy colours

USE AND CARE

Washing: Machine washable

Drying: Machine dryable

Notes: Warm iron

GENERAL QUALITIES

Look: Smooth and slightly mottled in coloration

Stitch definition: Good

Draping: Rayon improves the drape slightly

Pilling: No pilling

Resilience: Low

Durability: This is a highly durable fibre blend

Colour retention: Some fading will occur in the linen, whereas the rayon will hold its colour. A garment will take on an aged look after a few washes

Feel: Smooth and cool

Warmth: Low

Breathability: Good

Moisture resistance: Low

Moisture wicking: Rayon and linen together have high-moisture absorption qualities

Allergens and toxins: Low allergenic mix

Fire retardancy: Rayon reduces flammability

Sustainability: Poor; both fibres involve intensive processing and the heavy use of chemicals in their production

LINEN AND ALPACA

Alpaca is a warm and elastic fibre that creates a cosier yarn blend with a light halo. Linen adds a characteristic fleck and texture to the smooth alpaca, giving this blend a natural and rustic look. It is perfect for home interior designs and inter-season garments.

SPECS

Relative cost: An expensive yarn blend

Range of weights: 8 ply

Range of colours: Muted and light pastels; earthy and dark colours

USE AND CARE

Washing: Gentle machine wash

Drying: Dry flat to avoid warping from alpaca content

Notes: Gently steam to fluff up the nap of the alpaca

GENERAL QUALITIES

Look: Slightly crinkled with light halo

Stitch definition: Medium

Draping: Alpaca improves the drape in this yarn mix

Pilling: Alpaca increases tendency to pill

Resilience: Improved resilience with the addition of alpaca

Durability: High; a strong fibre combination

Colour retention: Will fade over time

Feel: Soft

Warmth: Temperate

Breathability: Good

Moisture resistance: Improved with the addition of alpaca

Moisture wicking: Highly moisture-absorbent

Allergens and toxins: Low allergy risk

Fire retardancy: Low flammability

Sustainability: Alpaca has a relatively low environmental impact and therefore improves the sustainability of this yarn blend

LINEN WEIGHTS

FINE LINEN

Fine linen is usually spun in a single ply and is perfect for lace knitting. It is stiff when first knitted, but it does soften when washed.

GAUGE AND YARDAGE GUIDE

WEIGHT	RECOMMENDED NEEDLE SIZE	YARDAGE PER 100g (yd / m)	GAUGE / TENSION (stitches and rows per 4in / 10cm)	CHEST (yd / m) 34–36in / 86–91cm	CHEST (yd / m) 38–40in / 97–101cm	CHEST (yd / m) 42–44in / 107–112cm	CHEST (yd / m) 46–48in / 117–122cm	WRAPS PER INCH
4 ply	2–4 / 2.75–3.5mm	350–400 / 320–365	25–27 and 35–39	1,500 / 1,370	1,800 / 1,650	2,100 / 1,920	2,400 / 2,195	19–21

4-ply 100% wet-spun linen on 4 / 3.5mm needles in stockinette / stocking stitch

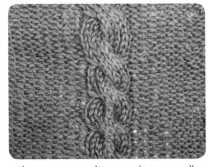

4-ply 100% wet-spun linen on 4 / 3.5mm needles in cable

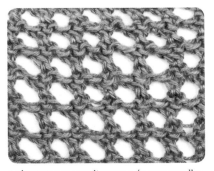

4-ply 100% wet-spun linen on 4 / 3.5mm needles in lace

MEDIUM LINEN

Medium-weight linen makes lovely light summer knitwear. It is not an easy yarn to knit with, as it is so inelastic; however, blending with other fibres makes it easier to handle. The slubby yarn in the swatches below has given the appearance of an uneven tension and magnified the ladder in the cable swatch.

GAUGE AND YARDAGE GUIDE

WEIGHT	RECOMMENDED NEEDLE SIZE	YARDAGE PER 100g (yd / m)	GAUGE / TENSION (stitches and rows per 4in / 10cm)	CHEST (yd / m) 34–36in / 86–91cm	CHEST (yd / m) 38–40in / 97–101cm	CHEST (yd / m) 42–44in / 107–112cm	CHEST (yd / m) 46–48in / 117–122cm	WRAPS PER INCH
5 ply	4–5 / 3.5–3.75mm	270–300 / 250–275	24–26 and 34–36	1,400 / 1,280	1,700 / 1,550	2,000 / 1,830	2,300 / 2,100	21–22
8 ply	4–6 / 3.5–4mm	200–250 / 180–230	20–22 and 28–30	1,300 / 1,190	1,600 / 1,460	1,900 / 1,740	2,200 / 2,010	19–20
10 ply	7 / 4.5mm	140–180 / 130–165	16–18 and 24–26	1,200 / 1,100	1,500 / 1,370	1,800 / 1,650	2,100 / 1,920	17–18

8-ply 55% viscose, 33% cotton, 12% linen on 8 / 5mm needles in stockinette / stocking stitch

8-ply 55% viscose, 33% cotton, 12% linen on 8 / 5mm needles in cable

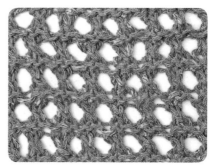

8-ply 55% viscose, 33% cotton, 12% linen on 8 / 5mm needles in lace

BULKY LINEN

Bulky linen is not very common, and is often mixed with other fibres. Linen can tend to drop a little under its own weight, as it has very little elasticity to help it spring back into shape. It is a good choice of yarn for chunky knits without excessive warmth.

GAUGE AND YARDAGE GUIDE

WEIGHT	RECOMMENDED NEEDLE SIZE	YARDAGE PER 100g (yd / m)	GAUGE / TENSION (stitches and rows per 4in / 10cm)	CHEST (yd / m) 34–36in / 86–91cm	CHEST (yd / m) 38–40in / 97–101cm	CHEST (yd / m) 42–44in / 107–112cm	CHEST (yd / m) 46–48in / 117–122cm	WRAPS PER INCH
12 ply	8–11 / 5–8mm	100–120 / 90–110	12–14 and 18–20	1,100 / 1,005	1,400 / 1,280	1,700 / 1,550	2,000 / 1,830	15–16

12-ply 50% linen, 50% cotton on 11 / 8mm needles in stockinette / stocking stitch

12-ply 50% linen, 50% cotton on 11 / 8mm needles in cable

12-ply 50% linen, 50% cotton on 11 / 8mm needles in lace

RAYON

Rayon is manmade, but, as a plant-derived cellulose, is considered a vegetable fibre, and provides a cheaper alternative to natural fibres, particularly silk. It is cool and shiny with plenty of drape. It is traditionally smooth and soft, and is often made into ribbon and tape yarns. It is highly absorbent, but does not insulate body heat, so it is perfect for cool summer knits. It is popular as a Medium-weight yarn in 8 ply. Because rayon is so slippery to knit with, it is sometimes spun as a bouclé or textured yarn.

SPECS

Source: Regenerated plant cellulose from wood pulp

Relative cost: An inexpensive fibre

Range of weights: 8 ply; less readily available in 3 ply

Range of colours: Diverse range of pastels and muted tones to bright hues

USE AND CARE

Washing: Check the belly band for washing instructions

Drying: Lay flat to dry

Notes: Cool iron and dry-cleanable

GENERAL QUALITIES

Look: Smooth and shiny

Stitch definition: Good

Draping: Good

Pilling: High pilling

Resilience: Low resilience as rayon is inelastic

Durability: Ages poorly; weakens with wear and discolours

Colour retention: High dye absorption

Feel: Cool and soft

Warmth: A low-warmth fibre

Breathability: Breathes well and conducts heat away from the body, making it a perfect summer yarn

Moisture resistance: High; however, tends to weaken when wet

Moisture wicking: It absorbs moisture readily, which makes a light, breathable fabric in warm weather

Allergens and toxins: Low allergy risk

Fire retardancy: Low flammability

Sustainability: This is a heavily processed fibre, which creates a great deal of environmental pollution

PROS

- ✔ Lightweight:
  Rayon is a light summer fibre

- ✔ Colours:
  Absorbs dye well and is available in a range
  of highly lustrous colours

- ✔ Drapes:
  Drapes well

- ✔ Comfort:
  Soft and comfortable against the skin

- ✔ Shrink-resistant:
  Some newly manufactured rayon yarns
  are created as shrink-resistant fibres

CONS

- ✔ Poor sustainability:
  This is a highly processed fibre that has a heavy
  environmental impact

- ✔ Wear:
  Ages poorly and weakens when wet

BURN TEST

Rayon burns rapidly and leaves only a slight ash.
It smells like burning leaves.

RAYON BLENDS

Rayon is often added to other fibres to reduce the price of and add softness to a yarn blend. It is also often used in blends to create novelty textured yarns such as ribbon, tape and bouclé, ideal for creating fashion-forward garments and accessories.

RAYON AND SILK

Rayon has all the comfort qualities of silk, but adds economy to this yarn blend. Silk improves the durability and adds warmth and luxury to this yarn. Depending on the silk, this yarn blend can range from smooth to textured. A rayon and silk mix is popularly spun as an 8-ply weight. This is a perfect yarn for making inter-season garments or light summer-weight lace knits.

SPECS

Relative cost: More expensive than a pure rayon blend

Range of weights: 8 ply; less readily available in 3 ply

Range of colours: Pastel and muted light tones to bright and jewel colours

USE AND CARE

Washing: Tepid and gentle machine-wash; avoid excessive agitation to avoid shrinkage

Drying: Dry flat to avoid warping

Notes: Warm iron

GENERAL QUALITIES

Look: Smooth and shiny

Stitch definition: High

Draping: Good

Pilling: Silk increases tendency to pill

Resilience: This yarn bland has low elasticity

Durability: Silk improves the durability of this mix

Colour retention: Good

Feel: Smooth and soft against the skin

Warmth: Temperate

Breathability: Good

Moisture resistance: High; the addition of silk improves the strength of this yarn blend when wet

Moisture wicking: High moisture-absorption qualities

Allergens and toxins: Low allergenic mix

Fire retardancy: Rayon reduces the flammability

Sustainability: Rayon is a heavily manufactured and chemically produced fibre. If mixed with ethically and environmentally produced silk, this improves the sustainability of the yarn

RAYON AND MOHAIR

Rayon is often blended with mohair to make a more cohesive yarn, binding mohair's furry fibres together and smoothing the feel against the skin. Mohair also adds warmth to this yarn blend and adds a halo to the surface texture. This yarn combination has a high lustre and comes in a wide range of shiny colours. As a novelty yarn it is often blended with dye variegates and metallic mixes, and is most often spun as a Medium-weight yarn. It is perfect for uncomplicated designs such as scarves to reveal the yarn's texture.

SPECS

Relative cost: More expensive than a pure rayon blend

Range of weights: 8 ply; less readily available in 3 ply

Range of colours: Muted and light pastels; earthy and dark colours

USE AND CARE

Washing: Check the belly band for washing instructions

Drying: Lay flat to dry to avoid excess warping

Notes: Gently steam to fluff up the mohair nap

GENERAL QUALITIES

Look: Shiny and textured, with halo

Stitch definition: Medium

Draping: Good

Pilling: Prone to pilling

Resilience: Low elasticity

Durability: Improved with the addition of mohair

Colour retention: Good colour

Feel: Furry against the skin

Warmth: Temperate

Breathability: Good

Moisture resistance: High

Moisture wicking: Highly moisture-absorbent

Allergens and toxins: Low allergy risk, although mohair's furry fibres may irritate the skin

Fire retardancy: Low flammability

Sustainability: Rayon is poor on the sustainability front; however, mohair can be produced as a sustainable farming enterprise, so this improves the eco status of this yarn blend

QUICK TIP

Rayon is an inelastic yarn, which can be challenging for achieving an even knitting tension. Knit small test swatches to become accustomed to working with it.

RAYON WEIGHTS

MEDIUM RAYON

Medium-weight rayon yarn is cool, so makes lovely summer-weight accessories such as wraps, throws and scarves, and garments such as cardigans and jumpers. It is an inelastic yarn to work with, but holds a lovely drape with a shiny surface texture.

GAUGE AND YARDAGE GUIDE

WEIGHT	RECOMMENDED NEEDLE SIZE	YARDAGE PER 100g (yd / m)	GAUGE / TENSION (stitches and rows per 4in / 10cm)	CHEST (yd / m) 34–36in / 86–91cm	CHEST (yd / m) 38–40in / 97–101cm	CHEST (yd / m) 42–44in / 107–112cm	CHEST (yd / m) 46–48in / 117–122cm	WRAPS PER INCH
8 ply	6 / 4mm	200–275 / 180–250	22–24 and 20–26	1,300 / 1,190	1,600 / 1,460	1,900 / 1,740	2,200 / 2,010	20

8-ply 100% rayon on 8 / 5mm needles in stockinette / stocking stitch

0 ply 100% rayon on 8 / 5mm needles in cable

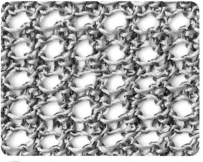

8-ply 100% rayon on 8 / 5mm needles in lace

BAMBOO

Bamboo is a cellulose fibre that is extracted from the bamboo plant. It is processed in two ways: naturally, in which the fibre is stripped, crushed and spun into yarn; and synthetically, in which the pulp extract is chemically treated to be spun into a viscose yarn. When naturally processed, bamboo is considered an eco fibre. It has a high lustre, and is soft, smooth and comfortable against the skin. It has thermo-regulating properties, keeping the wearer cool in summer and warm in winter. It is also hypoallergenic and anti-bacterial. Bamboo is a popular summer-weight yarn in 8 ply for light jumpers and cardigans, although other weights are available. It is often added to wool for bulkier-weight yarn, creating a moderately warm yarn blend. It is easily blended with other fibres to create fine yarns for lace knitting and accessories.

SPECS

Source: Bamboo plant

Relative cost: An inexpensive fibre

Range of weights: 3 ply to 10 ply

Range of colours: Diverse range of pastels and muted tones to bright hues

USE AND CARE

Washing: Handwash in tepid water. Avoid heat and agitation to prevent shrinkage

Drying: Dry flat, as bamboo can tend to warp

Notes: Reshape while wet

GENERAL QUALITIES

Look: Smooth and shiny

Stitch definition: Good

Draping: Good drape, but has tendency to over-drape

Pilling: Low pilling

Resilience: An inelastic fibre; holds shape well and drops with wear but recovers when washed

Durability: Good fibre strength

Colour retention: High dye absorption

Feel: Cool and soft

Warmth: A thermo-regulating fibre, providing insulation in the cold

Breathability: Breathes extremely well and conducts heat away from the body, making it a perfect summer yarn

Moisture resistance: Low

Moisture wicking: Bamboo absorbs moisture readily, which makes a light, breathable fabric in warm weather

Allergens and toxins: Low allergy risk and good for sensitive skin; kills germs and bacteria

Fire retardancy: Low flammability

Sustainability: Bamboo grows naturally without the use of pesticides. It is sustainably harvested, and is a biodegradable material. The processing of the fibre makes it debatable as to whether bamboo is an eco fibre, as its production is unregulated and can involve the use of chemicals resulting in post-industrial waste

PROS

- ✎ **Lightweight and breathable:**
  Bamboo is light and cool for summer knits
- ✎ **Comfort:**
  Soft, smooth and comfortable against the skin

CONS

- ✎ **Splitting:**
  Less cohesive than other natural fibres, bamboo can tend to split during knitting. Using blunt-ended needles may alleviate this tendency
- ✎ **Moisture absorption:**
  Can tend to weaken when wet as it holds so much moisture. Takes a long time to dry

QUICK TIP

Bamboo has an exquisite drape and is good for garments that benefit from this feature.

BURN TEST

Bamboo burns and chars and turns to soft grey ash, with the odour of burning grass. A bamboo and viscose mix will react in the same way but have the odour of burning paper.

BAMBOO BLENDS

Bamboo is often mixed with other fibres to add a silkiness and softness to fibres such as cotton and wool. This increases its versatility as it can be used for year-round yarns and for inter-season knitting.

BAMBOO AND COTTON

Bamboo adds a lovely drape, lustre and silkiness to cotton, making it an ideal summer yarn. Cotton adds economy to this yarn blend. It is a light yarn that breathes well in warm weather, with superb moisture-wicking properties for keeping the skin cool and dry. It is mostly spun in 5-ply, 8-ply, and 10-ply weights.

SPECS

Relative cost: An inexpensive fibre blend

Range of weights: 5 ply to 10 ply

Range of colours: Pastel and muted light tones, to bright and jewel colours

USE AND CARE

Washing: Gentle machine wash; dry-cleanable

Drying: Dry flat; do not tumble dry

Notes: Warm iron

GENERAL QUALITIES

Look: Smooth with high lustre

Stitch definition: High

Draping: Lovely drape

Pilling: Low pilling

Resilience: Low elasticity

Durability: Good

Colour retention: Good

Feel: Cool, smooth and soft against the skin

Warmth: Low

Breathability: Good

Moisture resistance: Low

Moisture wicking: High moisture-absorption qualities

Allergens and toxins: Low allergenic mix

Fire retardancy: Bamboo is less flammable than cotton, and reduces the risk of quick ignition

Sustainability: Bamboo and cotton are both highly processed fibres, produced with contaminating chemicals. If the bamboo is organically produced, its fibre is more ecologically sustainable

BAMBOO AND WOOL

Bamboo adds softness to wool, which is sometimes scratchy against the skin. It also adds a hypoallergenic and antibacterial benefit. Wool adds warmth, elasticity and buoyancy to this yarn blend, making it a good all-purpose, inter-season yarn mix. It is spun as Fine- and Medium-weight yarns, making it ideal for accessories such as socks, scarves, wraps and shawls. Medium-weight yarn bamboo and wool blends make great jumpers and cardigans. They are also available in 10-ply and 12-ply yarns.

SPECS

Relative cost: An inexpensive fibre blend

Range of weights: 3 ply to 12 ply

Range of colours: Muted and light pastels; earthy and dark colours

USE AND CARE

Washing: Gentle handwash in tepid water

Drying: Lay flat to dry

Notes: Can be machine-washed if mixed with superwash wool

GENERAL QUALITIES

Look: Light brush, high lustre

Stitch definition: Good

Draping: Good

Pilling: Prone to pilling

Resilience: Good elasticity with the addition of wool

Durability: Good

Colour retention: Good

Feel: Softer with the addition of bamboo

Warmth: Temperate

Breathability: Good

Moisture resistance: Improved with the addition of wool

Moisture wicking: Highly moisture-absorbent

Allergens and toxins: Bamboo reduces the allergy risk in this yarn blend

Fire retardancy: Low flammability

Sustainability: Bamboo, if naturally and organically produced, improves the sustainability of this yarn blend

BAMBOO WEIGHTS

FINE BAMBOO

Fine-weight bamboo is scarce, and is more often mixed with cotton or wool. It is more cohesive in a blend, with less tendency to split while knitting. Fine bamboo is a lovely yarn to use for lace knitting or light accessories, as it has a natural drape and breeziness.

GAUGE AND YARDAGE GUIDE

WEIGHT	RECOMMENDED NEEDLE SIZE	YARDAGE PER 100g (yd / m)	GAUGE / TENSION (stitches and rows per 4in / 10cm)	CHEST (yd / m) 34–36in / 86–91cm	CHEST (yd / m) 38–40in / 97–101cm	CHEST (yd / m) 42–44in / 107–112cm	CHEST (yd / m) 46–48in / 117–122cm	WRAPS PER INCH
3 ply	3–4 / 3.25–3.5mm	600–700 / 550–640	30–32 and 38–40	1,600 / 1,460	1,900 / 1,740	2,200 / 2,010	2,500 / 2,290	24–26
4 ply	4–5 / 3.5–3.75mm	500–550 / 460–500	28–32 and 32–36	1,500 / 1,370	1,800 / 1,650	2,100 / 1,920	2,400 / 2,195	22–23
5 ply	4–5 / 3.5–3.75mm	350–480 / 320–440	24–28 and 28–30	1,400 / 1,280	1,700 / 1,560	2,000 / 1,830	2,300 / 2,100	20–21

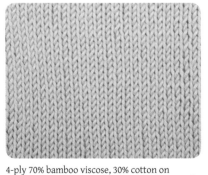

4-ply 70% bamboo viscose, 30% cotton on 4 / 3.5mm needles in stockinette / stocking stitch

4-ply 70% bamboo viscose, 30% cotton on 4 / 3.5mm needles in cable

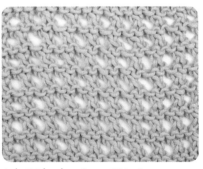

4-ply 70% bamboo viscose, 30% cotton on 4 / 3.5mm needles in lace

MEDIUM BAMBOO

Bamboo is available mostly in Medium weights, either as a pure fibre or mixed. It is an inelastic fibre, but has a beautiful drape and lightness, making it ideal for summer jumpers, cardigans and wraps.

GAUGE AND YARDAGE GUIDE

WEIGHT	RECOMMENDED NEEDLE SIZE	YARDAGE PER 100g (yd / m)	GAUGE / TENSION (stitches and rows per 4in / 10cm)	CHEST (yd / m) 34–36in / 86–91cm	CHEST (yd / m) 38–40in / 97–101cm	CHEST (yd / m) 42–44in / 107–112cm	CHEST (yd / m) 46–48in / 117–122cm	WRAPS PER INCH
8 ply	6 / 4mm	200–275 / 180–250	22–24 and 24–26	1,300 / 1,190	1,600 / 1,460	1,900 / 1,740	2,200 / 2,010	16–18
10 ply	7 / 4.5mm	170–190 / 155–175	18–20 and 20–22	1,200 / 1,100	1,500 / 1,370	1,800 / 1,650	2,100 / 1,920	12–14

8-ply 52% pima cotton, 48% bamboo on 8 / 5mm needles in stockinette / stocking stitch

8-ply 52% pima cotton, 48% bamboo on 8 / 5mm needles in cable

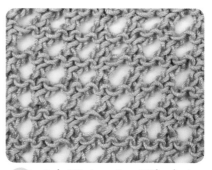

8-ply 52% pima cotton, 48% bamboo on 8 / 5mm needles in lace

BULKY BAMBOO

Bulky bamboo is often mixed with fibres such as cotton or wool to give bulkier yarns. As bamboo is so soft and has lots of drape, these other fibres help to add structure to the mix. Bulky bamboo is a good all-seasons yarn for a light garment that has bulk without too much warmth.

GAUGE AND YARDAGE GUIDE

WEIGHT	RECOMMENDED NEEDLE SIZE	YARDAGE PER 100g (yd / m)	GAUGE / TENSION (stitches and rows per 4in / 10cm)	CHEST (yd / m) 34–36in / 86–91cm	CHEST (yd / m) 38–40in / 97–101cm	CHEST (yd / m) 42–44in / 107–112cm	CHEST (yd / m) 46–48in / 117–122cm	WRAPS PER INCH
12 ply	8–9 / 5–5.5mm	140–150 / 130–135	14–16 and 16–18	1,100 / 1,005	1,300 / 1,190	1,700 / 1,550	2,000 / 1,830	8–10

12-ply 70% bamboo viscose, 30% wool on 10¹⁄₂–11 / 7mm needles in stockinette / stocking stitch

12-ply 70% bamboo viscose, 30% wool on 10¹⁄₂–11 / 7mm needles in cable

12-ply 70% bamboo viscose, 30% wool on 10¹⁄₂–11 / 7mm needles in lace

SOYA

Soya fibre is a plant protein fibre made from a by-product of the soybean. It is considered to be an eco fibre. It is a soft and luxurious yarn, and is lofty and cool, with a high lustre and soft drape. It is popular as a Medium-weight yarn in 8 ply, and is suitable for any item that hugs the skin, such as tank tops, jumpers, scarves and cardigans. Soya is also a hypoallergenic fibre and therefore good for babies' and children's knits. Soya blends well with other fibres, giving it more features and extending its application.

SPECS

Source: Soybean

Relative cost: An expensive fibre

Range of weights: 8 ply

Range of colours: Undyed, it is ivory-coloured; dyed, it is available in a wide range of colours from pastels to bright colours

USE AND CARE

Washing: Machine-wash and dry on gentle cycle

Drying: Machine-dry on gentle cycle

Notes: Warm iron

GENERAL QUALITIES

Look: Smooth with high lustre

Stitch definition: Good

Draping: Good

Pilling: Low pilling

Resilience: An inelastic fibre

Durability: Good fibre strength

Colour retention: High dye absorption

Feel: Soft and cool

Warmth: Temperate

Breathability: Breathes extremely well

Moisture resistance: Low

Moisture wicking: Absorbs moisture readily

Allergens and toxins: Low allergy risk and good for sensitive skin

Fire retardancy: Low flammability

Sustainability: Soya fibre is considered an eco and organic fibre. It is produced from the waste of soybean production

PROS

✎ **Lustre:**
Soy fibre has the lustre of silk with beautiful drape

✎ **Comfort:**
The fibre is soft, smooth and lightweight

✎ **Absorbency:**
Soy has good moisture absorption and
moisture transmission

✎ **Easy-care:**
Shrink- and crease-resistant

CONS

✎ **Moderate elasticity:**
Soya is not an elastic yarn and can drop
when knitted

BURN TEST

Soya burns and chars, and smells of burning grass.
It will leave a soft grey ash.

QUICK TIP

As soya yarn tends to drop a little when knitting,
it is a good idea to keep tension firm by using
smaller needles than recommended.

SOYA BLENDS

Bamboo is often mixed with other fibres to add a silkiness and softness to fibres such as cotton and wool. This increases its versatility as it can be used for year-round yarns and for inter-season knitting.

SOYA AND COTTON

Soya is commonly blended with cotton to reduce its price. This blend is an ideal summer yarn, with soya adding lightness to cotton, which tends to over-drape from its own weight. Soya also adds a lustre and luxuriousness to cotton, improving its handle and feel against the skin. It is perfect for making airy shawls and summer-weight garments.

SPECS

Relative cost: An inexpensive fibre blend

Range of weights: 8 ply

Range of colours: Pastel and muted light tones, to bright and jewel colours

USE AND CARE

Washing: Gently machine-wash; dry-cleanable

Drying: Machine-dryable on gentle cycle

Notes: Warm iron

GENERAL QUALITIES

Look: Smooth, lightly brushed and medium lustre

Stitch definition: High

Draping: Lovely drape; will drop with wear, but recovers when washed

Pilling: Prone to pilling from the cotton

Resilience: Low elasticity in this yarn blend

Durability: Good

Colour retention: Good

Feel: Cool, smooth and soft against the skin

Warmth: Low warmth

Breathability: Good

Moisture resistance: Low

Moisture wicking: High moisture-absorption qualities

Allergens and toxins: Low allergenic mix

Fire retardancy: Soya reduces flammability

Sustainability: Soya improves the sustainability of this blend

SOYA AND BAMBOO

This is an extremely soft yarn combination, with hypoallergenic and antibacterial benefit. It is perfect for babies' and children's knits.

SPECS

Relative cost: An affordable yarn blend

Range of weights: 8 ply

Range of colours: Muted and light pastels to bright and dark colours

USE AND CARE

Washing: Handwash in tepid water

Drying: Lay flat to dry to avoid warping

Notes: Avoid heat agitation to prevent shrinkage

GENERAL QUALITIES

Look: Light brush, high lustre

Stitch definition: Good

Draping: Good

Pilling: Low pilling

Resilience: Low elasticity

Durability: Good

Colour retention: Good

Feel: Soft and cool

Warmth: Temperate

Breathability: Good

Moisture resistance: Low

Moisture wicking: Highly moisture-absorbent

Allergens and toxins: A low-allergy blend

Fire retardancy: Low flammability

Sustainability: Soya, being produced from waste product, is fairly sustainable. Bamboo is questionably sustainable as, although it is grown organically and requires little water, there are no regulations protecting cheap labour production. A bamboo/soya blend is not proven as sustainable

SOYA WEIGHTS

MEDIUM SOYA

Soya is available mostly in Medium-weight yarns, both as a pure fibre or mixed with other fibres in yarn blends.
It is an inelastic fibre, but has a beautiful drape and lightness, making it ideal for summer jumpers, cardigans and wraps.

GAUGE AND YARDAGE GUIDE

WEIGHT	RECOMMENDED NEEDLE SIZE	YARDAGE PER 100g (yd / m)	GAUGE / TENSION (stitches and rows per 4in / 10cm)	CHEST (yd / m) 34–36in / 86–91cm	CHEST (yd / m) 38–40in / 97–101cm	CHEST (yd / m) 42–44in / 107–112cm	CHEST (yd / m) 46–48in / 117–122cm	WRAPS PER INCH
8 ply	4–7 / 3.5–4.5mm	200–275 / 180–250	22–24 and 25–28	1,300 / 1,190	1,600 / 1,460	1,900 / 1,740	2,200 / 2,010	16

8-ply 55% bamboo, 45% soya on 7 / 4.5mm noodles in stockinette / stocking stitch

8-ply 55% bamboo, 45% soya on 7 / 4.5mm needles in cable

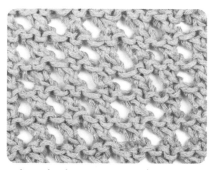

8-ply 55% bamboo, 45% soya on 7 / 4.5mm needles in lace

HEMP

Hemp is a cellulose bast fibre derived from the cannabis plant. It is a soft, durable fibre that dyes well, resists mildew, is ultraviolet-resistant and has natural antibacterial properties. Hemp fibre is considered an eco fibre as it grows quickly and abundantly without the use of pesticides and the need for heavy irrigation. Hemp is a good all-seasons yarn that is cool in summer and warm in winter. It is usually available as a Fine- or Medium-weight yarn, from 4 ply to 8 ply. It is also often mixed with other fibres, as it is strong and versatile.

SPECS

Source: Bast fibre from the *Cannabis genus* plant

Relative cost: An inexpensive fibre

Range of weights: 4 ply to 8 ply

Range of colours: Undyed hemp ranges from creamy white and brown to grey, black, or green. Dyed, it comes in a variety of muted and earthy colours and bright tones

USE AND CARE

Washing: Machine-washable

Drying: Lay flat to dry

Notes: Reshape while damp; hemp softens with each launder

GENERAL QUALITIES

Look: Smooth, mid-sheen and light brush

Stitch definition: Good

Draping: Good

Pilling: Low pilling

Resilience: Low elasticity

Durability: Very strong

Colour retention: High dye absorption

Feel: Soft

Warmth: Temperate and temperature-regulating

Breathability: Breathes well

Moisture resistance: High

Moisture wicking: It absorbs moisture readily

Allergens and toxins: Low allergy risk; hemp is an antibacterial fibre and is mould-resistant

Fire retardancy: Low flammability

Sustainability: Hemp is a renewable resource, and is a biodegradable and organically produced fibre. It grows quickly without the use of pesticides or heavy irrigation

PROS

- **Soft:**
  Hemp's softness and wearability improves with washing and the fibre ages well
- **Drapes:**
  Drapes well
- **Comfort:**
  Soft and comfortable against the skin
- **Low shrinkage:**
  Hemp is shrink-, pilling- and stretch-resistant

CONS

- **Stiffness:**
  Some hemp yarn spins can be stiff to knit with if wet-spun as a pure fibre blend, although hemp will soften with washing and wearing

BURN TEST

Hemp burns quickly with a bright flame. It leaves no melted bead and smells like burning leaves or wood. The ash is grey and the smoke has no fume hazard.

QUICK TIP

Hemp is sometimes wet-spun with a starch coating, like linen. This may make it stiff to knit with, but soaking and washing the knitted items brings out the fibre's softness, which improves even more with further washing.

HEMP BLENDS

Hemp is often mixed with other fibres, as it is so versatile and strong. It is a long fibre, which can adapt to many different types of yarn spins. It is a good inter-season fibre as it is temperature-regulating.

HEMP AND WOOL

Hemp softens the feel of wool against the skin and improves the hypoallergenic benefit in this yarn blend. Wool adds elasticity and buoyancy to the mix. It is popular as an 8-ply yarn weight. Wool adds warmth to this blend, but not too much, making it suitable for inter-season garments and accessories.

SPECS

Relative cost: An inexpensive yarn blend

Range of weights: 4 ply to 8 ply

Range of colours: Pastel and muted light tones, to bright and jewel colours

USE AND CARE

Washing: The addition of hemp makes this fibre mix machine-washable as long as the wool is superwash. Avoid excessive agitation to avoid shrinkage in case the wool is not superwash

Drying: Dry flat to avoid warping

Notes: Warm iron

GENERAL QUALITIES

Look: Smooth and mid-sheen, light brush

Stitch definition: High

Draping: Good

Pilling: Hemp reduces the tendency to pill

Resilience: Wool improves elasticity

Durability: Hemp improves durability

Colour retention: Good colour retention

Feel: Smooth and soft against the skin

Warmth: Temperate

Breathability: Good

Moisture resistance: High

Moisture wicking: High moisture-absorption qualities

Allergens and toxins: Low allergenic mix

Fire retardancy: Low flammability

Sustainability: A good sustainable blend, particularly if the wool is organic and not heavily processed

HEMP AND CASHMERE

Hemp is blended with cashmere to add durability and economy to this yarn. Cashmere adds luxury and elasticity. The softness of both fibres creates an affordable luxury yarn with lightness, drape and a lovely lustre. It is an ideal blend for making inter-season jumpers, cardigans and accessories.

SPECS

Relative cost: More expensive than pure hemp

Range of weights: 4 ply to 8 ply

Range of colours: Muted and light pastels; earthy and dark colours

USE AND CARE

Washing: Gentle handwash in tepid water

Drying: Lay flat to dry to avoid warping

Notes: Dry-cleanable

GENERAL QUALITIES

Look: Light sheen with soft halo

Stitch definition: Medium

Draping: Good

Pilling: Low pilling

Resilience: Good elasticity

Durability: Improved with the addition of hemp

Colour retention: Good

Feel: Soft against the skin

Warmth: Temperate

Breathability: Good

Moisture resistance: High

Moisture wicking: Highly moisture-absorbent

Allergens and toxins: Low allergy risk

Fire retardancy: Low flammability

Sustainability: Good

HEMP WEIGHTS

FINE HEMP

Fine hemp is perfect for knitting lightweight shawls and wraps. It is a fairly inelastic yarn and can be sometimes difficult to knit with, but the softness that develops gradually over time makes it worth it. You can see the effect of a thinner section of yarn, due to an uneven spin, in the stockinette / stocking stitch swatch below.

GAUGE AND YARDAGE GUIDE

WEIGHT	RECOMMENDED NEEDLE SIZE	YARDAGE PER 100g (yd / m)	GAUGE / TENSION (stitches and rows per 4in / 10cm)	CHEST (yd / m) 34–36in / 86–91cm	CHEST (yd / m) 38–40in / 97–101cm	CHEST (yd / m) 42–44in / 107–112cm	CHEST (yd / m) 46–48in / 117–122cm	WRAPS PER INCH
4 ply	2–4 / 2.75–3.5mm	350–400 / 320–365	25–27 and 30–36	1,500 / 1,370	1,800 / 1,650	2,100 / 1,920	2,400 / 2,195	22–24
5 ply	4–5 / 3.5–3.75mm	270–300 / 250–275	24–26 and 27–29	1,400 / 1,280	1,700 / 1,550	2,000 / 1,830	2,300 / 2,100	19–21

5-ply 100% long-fibre hemp on 4 / 3.5mm needles in stockinette / stocking stitch

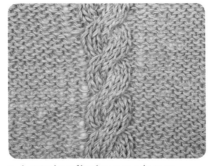

5-ply 100% long-fibre hemp on 4 / 3.5mm needles in cable

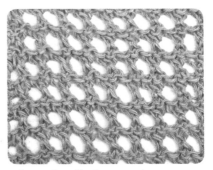

5-ply 100% long-fibre hemp on 4 / 3.5mm needles in lace

MEDIUM HEMP

Medium hemp yarn makes great lightweight garments with a little warmth. In yarn blends, hemp is temperature-regulating, making it versatile and suitable for many uses. It knits up beautifully and has good stitch definition, making it a good choice for showcasing fancy knitting stitches.

GAUGE AND YARDAGE GUIDE

WEIGHT	RECOMMENDED NEEDLE SIZE	YARDAGE PER 100g (yd / m)	GAUGE / TENSION (stitches and rows per 4in / 10cm)	CHEST (yd / m) 34–36in / 86–91cm	CHEST (yd / m) 38–40in / 97–101cm	CHEST (yd / m) 42–44in / 107–112cm	CHEST (yd / m) 46–48in / 117–122cm	WRAPS PER INCH
8 ply	4–6 / 3.5–4mm	200–250 / 180–230	20–22 and 24–26	1,300 / 1,190	1,600 / 1,460	1,900 / 1,740	2,200 / 2,010	16–18

8-ply 100% hemp on 8 / 5mm needles in stockinette / stocking stitch

8-ply 100% hemp on 8 / 5mm needles in cable

8-ply 100% hemp on 8 / 5mm needles in lace

RAMIE

Ramie is a bast fibre from the White China plant—a flowering plant from the nettle family. Ramie is a very long, fine fibre with a silky lustre, which improves with washing. Ramie is considered an exotic fibre, and is highly processed like linen, making it an expensive natural fibre. It is hypoallergenic and is ideal for summer-weight knits because of its high absorbency. Ramie is available in 1-ply and 2-ply Fine-weight yarn. It is an inelastic yarn that is particularly suitable for lace knitting as it holds its shape very well.

SPECS

Source: Bast fibre from *Boehmeria nivea*, the White China plant

Relative cost: An expensive fibre

Range of weights: 1 ply to 2 ply

Range of colours: Undyed, ramie is white and does not need bleaching. It also comes dyed in a range of natural plant dyes

USE AND CARE

Washing: Machine-wash on gentle cycle

Drying: Dry flat

Notes: Warm iron

GENERAL QUALITIES

Look: Lightly brushed with high lustre

Stitch definition: Good

Draping: Low drape as it is quite a stiff yarn

Pilling: Low pilling

Resilience: An inelastic fibre

Durability: Very strong fibre

Colour retention: High dye absorption

Feel: Soft and cool

Warmth: Low

Breathability: Breathes extremely well

Moisture resistance: High

Moisture wicking: High absorbency; ramie does not stick to the skin, making it very comfortable to wear in hot weather

Allergens and toxins: Low allergy risk and good for sensitive skin

Fire retardancy: Low flammability

Sustainability: Ramie is heavily processed to turn it into fibre, therefore making it less sustainable than many natural fibres

QUICK TIP

Because ramie is inelastic and stiff, it can be difficult to work with. Using wooden needles may make this easier. When ramie is knitted up it will take on a three-dimensional effect. It softens up beautifully when washed. Its softness and lustre improves with repeated washing over time.

PROS

🪡 **Lustre:**
Ramie has a natural high lustre

🪡 **Absorbency:**
Ramie has high absorption and moisture wicking

🪡 **Strength:**
The strongest of natural fibres

🪡 **Shrink-resistant:**
Ramie is shrink-resistant

CONS

🪡 **Low elasticity:**
Low elasticity and resilience

🪡 **Stiffness:**
Can be stiff and brittle; fibres will weaken
if creased in the same fold regularly

BURN TEST

Ramie burns and chars, and smells of burning grass.

RAMIE BLENDS

Ramie is a popular knitting yarn in Japan, but is still in scarce supply elsewhere. Ramie blends are even scarcer. However, if you are lucky enough to come across a ramie and wool blend, this is a light yarn with minimal shrinkage. A ramie and cotton blend has more lustre, strength and colour than a pure ramie.

RAMIE WEIGHTS

FINE RAMIE

Fine ramie is particularly good for lace knitting and lightweight accessories such as shawls and wraps. It is stiff and three-dimensional when first knitted, but softens with washing. It is an expensive yarn, but as it is a Fine yarn it has a generous yardage, which brings good value to a project.

GAUGE AND YARDAGE GUIDE

WEIGHT	RECOMMENDED NEEDLE SIZE	YARDAGE PER 100g (yd / m)	GAUGE / TENSION (stitches and rows per 4in / 10cm)	CHEST (yd / m) 34–36in / 86–91cm	CHEST (yd / m) 38–40in / 97–101cm	CHEST (yd / m) 42–44in / 107–112cm	CHEST (yd / m) 46–48in / 117–122cm	WRAPS PER INCH
1 ply	0–1 / 2–2.25mm	1,500–1,600 / 1,380–1,460	36–38 and 40–44	1,800 / 1,650	2,100 / 1,920	2,400 / 2,200	2,700 / 2,470	48–52
2 ply	1–2 / 2.25–2.75mm	1,200 –1,300 / 1,100–1,190	34–36 and 29–33	1,700 / 1,560	2,000 / 1,830	2,300 / 2,100	2,600 / 2,380	42–46

2-ply 100% ramie on 2–3 / 3mm needles in stockinette / stocking stitch

2-ply 100% ramie on 2–3 / 3mm needles in cable

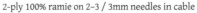

2-ply 100% ramie on 2–3 / 3mm needles in lace

TENCEL

Tencel is a cellulose fibre made from regenerated wood pulp. It is processed and spun like rayon, and, like rayon, is considered a cheaper alternative to silk. It has good strength, lustrous sheen, soft handle and a lovely drape. It is temperature regulating, so is cool in hot weather and warm in cold weather. It is a hypoallergenic fibre and is usually available as a blend with wool or cotton to create easy-care, trans-seasonal yarns. Tencel is available in Fine-weight yarns in 2 ply or 5 ply, and in Medium-weight yarns as 8 ply or 10 ply. It is often mixed with other fibres, such as cotton or wool, to form a Bulky yarn blend. It comes in a wide range of colours, and is a versatile yarn, suitable for babies', children's and adults' knits.

SPECS

Source: Wood pulp

Relative cost: Generally an inexpensive fibre, although more expensive than cotton and rayon

Range of weights: 2 ply to 12 ply

Range of colours: Pastels to bright hues

USE AND CARE

Washing: Machine-wash on gentle cycle

Drying: Machine-dry on gentle cycle

Notes: Cool iron

GENERAL QUALITIES

Look: Smooth with high lustre

Stitch definition: Good

Draping: Good

Pilling: Low pilling

Resilience: Moderate elasticity

Durability: Good fibre strength

Colour retention: High dye absorption

Feel: Soft and silky

Warmth: Temperate

Breathability: Breathes extremely well

Moisture resistance: High

Moisture wicking: Absorbs moisture readily

Allergens and toxins: Low allergy risk and good for sensitive skin

Fire retardancy: Low flammability

Sustainability: Tencel fibre is biodegradable, and is produced from sustainably managed timber; however, it is a heavily processed fibre requiring the heavy use of chemicals

PROS

- **Lustre:**
  Tencel fibre has the lustre of silk with beautiful drape

- **Comfort:**
  The fibre is soft, smooth and lightweight

- **Absorbency:**
  Tencel has good moisture absorption and moisture transmission

- **Easy-care:**
  Shrink- and crease-resistant

CONS

- **Slippery:**
  Tencel is a slippery yarn to work with, although it is more manageable as a blend

BURN TEST

Tencel burns and chars, and smells of burning wood. It will leave a soft grey ash.

TENCEL BLENDS

Tencel is often blended with cotton to make a cool summer yarn and with wool or alpaca to make warmer yarns. Tencel smooths the surface in these yarn mixes, improving durability and ease of care.

TENCEL AND COTTON

This yarn blend is light and perfect as a summer yarn, as it has good moisture-wicking qualities. Tencel adds a lustre and luxurious feel to this blend. It is perfect for making airy shawls and summer-weight garments.

SPECS

Relative cost: More expensive than a pure cotton blend
Range of weights: 8 ply to 12 ply
Range of colours: Pastels and muted light tones, to bright and jewel colours

USE AND CARE

Washing: Gentle machine-wash, dry cleanable
Drying: Lay flat to dry
Notes: Warm iron

GENERAL QUALITIES

Look: Smooth, lightly brushed, and medium lustre
Stitch definition: High
Draping: Lovely drape; will drop with wear, but recover when washed
Pilling: Prone to pilling from the cotton
Resilience: Low elasticity in this yarn blend
Durability: Good
Colour retention: Good
Feel: Cool, smooth and soft against the skin
Warmth: Low
Breathability: Good
Moisture resistance: High
Moisture wicking: High moisture-absorption qualities
Allergens and toxins: Low allergenic mix
Fire retardancy: Tencel reduces flammability
Sustainability: Tencel improves the sustainability of cotton

TENCEL AND WOOL

Tencel adds softness to this yarn blend, as wool can sometimes be scratchy against the skin. It also adds a hypoallergenic and antibacterial benefit. It is a good yarn for knitting trans-seasonal garments as Tencel cools the yarn in warmer weather. It is mostly available in 8 ply and 10 ply weights, suitable for shawls, wraps, jumpers and cardigans.

SPECS

Relative cost: An inexpensive fibre blend

Range of weights: 8 ply and 10 ply

Range of colours: Muted and light pastels to bright and dark colours

USE AND CARE

Washing: Handwash in tepid water

Drying: Lay flat to dry

Notes: Avoid heat agitation to prevent shrinkage

GENERAL QUALITIES

Look: Light brush, high lustre

Stitch definition: Good

Draping: Good

Pilling: Tencel reduces pilling in this yarn mix

Resilience: Good elasticity

Durability: Good

Colour retention: Good

Feel: Soft and light

Warmth: Temperate

Breathability: Good

Moisture resistance: High

Moisture wicking: Highly moisture absorbent

Allergens and toxins: Tencel reduces the risk of skin irritation

Fire retardancy: Low flammability

Sustainability: A good eco blend if the wool is organic

TENCEL WEIGHTS

FINE TENCEL

Fine tencel is generally mixed with other fibres to create smoother, silkier, Fine-weight yarns. These yarn mixes are perfect for lace knitting for shawls and wraps, as they have lovely drape but still hold their shape well.

GAUGE AND YARDAGE GUIDE

WEIGHT	RECOMMENDED NEEDLE SIZE	YARDAGE PER 100g (yd / m)	GAUGE / TENSION (stitches and rows per 4in / 10cm)	CHEST (yd / m) 34–36in / 86–91cm	CHEST (yd / m) 38–40in / 97–101cm	CHEST (yd / m) 42–44in / 107–112cm	CHEST (yd / m) 46–48in / 117–122cm	WRAPS PER INCH
2–3 ply	0–2 / 2–2.75mm	800–1,000 / 730–910	28–30 and 36–39	1,500 / 1,370	1,800 / 1,645	2,100 / 1,920	2,400 / 2,190	30–32
5 ply	5–6 / 3.75–4mm	250–400 / 230–365	24–26 and 32–34	1,200 / 1,100	1,500 / 1,370	1,800 / 1,645	2,100 / 1,920	26–28

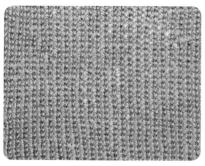

3-ply 100% tencel on 1 / 2.25mm needles in stockinette / stocking stitch

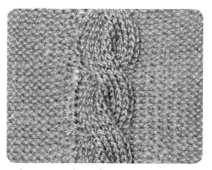

3-ply 100% tencel on 1 / 2.25mm needles in cable

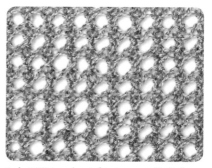

3-ply 100% tencel on 1 / 2.25mm needles in lace

MEDIUM TENCEL

Tencel is usually a mixed fibre in this yarn weight, making it suitable for all-seasons knitting for accessories and garments. This yarn weight has a lovely manageable drape.

GAUGE AND YARDAGE GUIDE

WEIGHT	RECOMMENDED NEEDLE SIZE	YARDAGE PER 100g (yd / m)	GAUGE / TENSION (stitches and rows per 4in / 10cm)	CHEST (yd / m) 34–36in / 86–91cm	CHEST (yd / m) 38–40in / 97–101cm	CHEST (yd / m) 42–44in / 107–112cm	CHEST (yd / m) 46–48in / 117–122cm	WRAPS PER INCH
8 ply	6 / 4mm	200–275 / 180–250	22–24 and 23–24	1,100 / 1,005	1,400 / 1,280	1,700 / 1,550	2,000 / 1,830	22–24
10 ply	7 / 4.5mm	170–190 / 155–175	18–20 and 20–22	1,000 / 915	1,300 / 1,190	1,600 / 1,460	1,900 / 1,740	18–20

8-ply 50% pima cotton, 50% tencel on 7 / 4.5mm needles in stockinette / stocking stitch

8-ply 50% pima cotton, 50% tencel on 7 / 4.5mm needles in cable

8-ply 50% pima cotton, 50% tencel on 7 / 4.5mm needles in lace

BULKY TENCEL

Tencel is usually a mixed fibre in this yarn weight, and is a good yarn choice for bulk without excessive warmth. It offers good stitch definition for cables, ribs and honeycomb stitches.

GAUGE AND YARDAGE GUIDE

WEIGHT	RECOMMENDED NEEDLE SIZE	YARDAGE PER 100g (yd / m)	GAUGE / TENSION (stitches and rows per 4in / 10cm)	CHEST (yd / m) 34–36in / 86–91cm	CHEST (yd / m) 38–40in / 97–101cm	CHEST (yd / m) 42–44in / 107–112cm	CHEST (yd / m) 46–48in / 117–122cm	WRAPS PER INCH
12 ply	10½–11 / 7mm	180–200 / 165–180	16–18 and 18–20	1,000 / 915	1,300 / 1,190	1,600 / 1,460	1,900 / 1,740	12–16

12-ply 50% pima cotton, 50% tencel on 10½–11 / 7mm needles in stockinette / stocking stitch

12-ply 50% pima cotton, 50% tencel on 10½–11 / 7mm needles in cable

12-ply 50% pima cotton, 50% tencel on 10½–11 / 7mm needles in lace

NYLON

Nylon, like polyester and acrylic, is derived from petroleum-based thermoplastics, and is also manufactured by a heat-bonding, filament-extrusion and melt-spin process. It is the manufacturers' secret formulas and additives that determine the differences between these synthetic fibres in appearance and character.

Nylon is also referred to as polyamide. It was first manufactured as a cheaper alternative to silk, but is now also spun as a high-fashion fancy yarn in a wide array of textures and mixes. Nylon is often blended with natural fibres to create all-purpose yarns.

SPECS

Source: Thermoplastic

Relative cost: Cheaper than natural fibres

Range of weights: 2 ply to 14 ply

Range of colours: Vast, ranging from light pastels to bright and deep colours

USE AND CARE

Washing: Can be machine-washed in warm or cold water on normal cycles

Drying: Can be tumble-dried at low temperatures

Notes: Do not iron

GENERAL QUALITIES

Look: Smooth and shiny

Stitch definition: High, unless in feather or eyelash yarns

Draping: High

Pilling: Low

Resilience: A high-elasticity, high-performance fibre

Durability: Strong and highly durable

Colour retention: High retention and lustrous shade depth

Feel: Cool on the skin

Warmth: Low

Breathability: Low breathability, but good wind resistance

Moisture resistance: Good water-resistance; a good weatherproof fibre

Moisture wicking: Rapid moisture-wicking properties

Allergens and toxins: Regarded as a low-irritant and hypoallergenic fibre

Fire retardancy: Nylon melts and then burns only at an extremely high temperature, giving it a lower flammability than natural fibres

Sustainability: Nylon, being made from petroleum, is fossil-fuel-dependent and emits nitrous oxide into the atmosphere. Recent recycling innovations have improved this, with the manufacturing process using as little as 15% of the production energy required for virgin nylon fibre

PROS

- **Soft and lightweight:**
  Non-abrasive and scratch-free, with a high loft

- **Easy-care:**
  Easy to launder; it is crease- and shrinkproof and can be washed and dried by machine

- **Durable:**
  Very wear-and-tear-resistant. Nylon is resilient, strong and elastic, and retains its shape

- **Lustre/Sheen:**
  Superior colour-fastness and high colour diversification

- **Shed-free:**
  Does not shed like natural fibres

CONS

- **Static:**
  Although nylon is soft, its tactility is artificial and it can feel static against the skin

- **Non-breathable:**
  Doesn't have the breathable qualities of a natural fibre

- **Non-sustainable:**
  The manufacturing of nylon poses an environmental risk

BURN TEST

Nylon melts and then burns rapidly. It smells like burning plastic.

NYLON BLENDS

Nylon is a light, synthetic fibre with a silky touch. It is often added to natural fibres to provide a lower-cost yarn, and its use in these blends can also improve the performance of a natural fibre, particularly its ease of care and durability. Synthetic blends with nylon—such as tube, tape, polar and fleece novelty yarns—come in a vast range of ever-changing fashion styles and palettes.

NYLON AND ALPACA

The addition of nylon to alpaca creates a light, strong yarn ideal for high-performance items such as socks, gloves and weatherproof garments. Nylon reduces alpaca's shedding, smooths out any scratchiness in it, and adds its stain-resistant qualities to the yarn.

SPECS

Relative cost: Less expensive than a pure alpaca blend

Range of weights: 2 ply to 6 ply

Range of colours: Natural and earthy greys and beiges; soft and muted pastels; deep autumnal tones

USE AND CARE

Washing: Nylon creates a more easy-care yarn; however, gentle machine cycles or handwashing are recommended to avoid any shrinkage

Drying: Dry flat

Notes: Dry-cleanable

GENERAL QUALITIES

Look: Light and fluffy

Stitch definition: Medium; alpaca gives some surface texture, and the nylon is often barely visible

Draping: Low, as both fibres are light

Pilling: Medium

Resilience: Nylon adds superior abrasion-resistance and high flexibility to alpaca, which already has high elasticity and good memory

Durability: High

Colour retention: The high colour retention of nylon improves the lustre of this blend

Feel: Soft and light

Warmth: Alpaca is very warm while nylon is cooling, creating a good balance

Breathability: Medium, as nylon reduces the breathability in this yarn blend

Moisture resistance: Both nylon and alpaca are water-resistant

Moisture wicking: Nylon adds moisture-wicking properties, which alpaca fibre lacks

Allergens and toxins: Low

Fire retardancy: Low

Sustainability: Alpaca improves the sustainability of this blend, as alpaca farming has a low environmental impact. This can be a sustainable yarn if the nylon is recycled

NYLON AND ACRYLIC

The blend of these two synthetic fibres creates a light and spongy fabric. It is available in fancy textures such as ribbon or tape yarn, but is generally supplied in a Medium-weight 5 ply or a Bulky 12–14-ply weight. This blend is usually easy to work with unless in a textured mix, in which case it can split or snag while knitting. It is cool against the skin and, being a high-fashion yarn, is a good choice for quick and stylish knits.

SPECS

Relative cost: An inexpensive blend

Range of weights: 2 ply to 14 ply

Range of colours: A vast range of colours and also textures, from super-shiny and glossy finishes to faux suedes and leather looks

USE AND CARE

Washing: This blend can be machine-washed

Drying: This blend can be machine-dried

Notes: Do not iron

GENERAL QUALITIES

Look: Varies from smooth to knobbly

Stitch definition: High with smooth yarns; low with textured yarns

Draping: This blend has a strong and spongy elasticity that is good for body-hugging fits

Pilling: Low

Resilience: Extremely high

Durability: High tensile strength

Colour retention: High; this yarn will not fade

Feel: Cool and spongy

Warmth: Low; has a cool synthetic texture

Breathability: Low

Moisture resistance: High and with good wind-resistance

Moisture wicking: Good

Allergens and toxins: Low

Fire retardancy: Low

Sustainability: Low

NYLON WEIGHTS

FINE NYLON

Fine nylon is an economical alternative for baby knits, as it is very soft and easy-care. A microfibre nylon is often blended with other fine natural fibres to add these benefits, and also to enhance durability. Nylon also has excellent moisture resistance and is a practical yarn for lightweight hats, wraps and scarves. It is easy to knit with.

GAUGE AND YARDAGE GUIDE

WEIGHT	RECOMMENDED NEEDLE SIZE	YARDAGE PER 100g (yd / m)	GAUGE / TENSION (stitches and rows per 4in / 10cm)	CHEST (yd / m) 34–36in / 86–91cm	CHEST (yd / m) 38–40in / 97–101cm	CHEST (yd / m) 42–44in / 107–112cm	CHEST (yd / m) 46–48in / 117–122cm	WRAPS PER INCH
2 ply	2–3 / 2.75–3.25mm	800–900 / 730–825	30–32 and 28–30	1,800 / 1,650	2,100 / 1,920	2,400 / 2,195	2,700 / 2,468	40–44
3 ply	4–6 / 3.5–4mm	700–800 / 640–730	26–28 and 25–27	1,700 / 1,554	2,000 / 1,830	2,300 / 2,105	2,600 / 2,380	34–38
4–5 ply	8–9 / 5–5.5mm	500–600 / 460–550	20–24 and 23–24	1,600 / 1,460	1,800 / 1,650	2,100 / 1,920	2,400 / 2,195	30–34

4-ply 55% nylon, 45% acrylic on 3 / 3.25mm needles in stockinette / stocking stitch

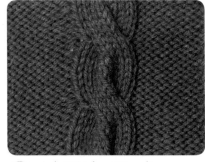

4-ply 55% nylon, 45% acrylic on 3 / 3.25mm needles in cable

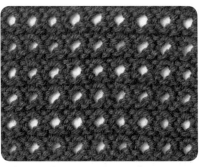

4-ply 55% nylon, 45% acrylic on 3 / 3.25mm needles in lace

MEDIUM NYLON

Medium-gauge nylon and nylon blends make hard-wearing yarn. Nylon is popular as a sock yarn because of its elasticity and durability. Its easy-care quality also makes it good for children's clothing and hard-wearing garments. Nylon fashion yarns in tape and ribbon spins have great buoyancy and work well for stretchy fashions.

GAUGE AND YARDAGE GUIDE

WEIGHT	RECOMMENDED NEEDLE SIZE	YARDAGE PER 100g (yd / m)	GAUGE / TENSION (stitches and rows per 4in / 10cm)	CHEST (yd / m) 34–36in / 86–91cm	CHEST (yd / m) 38–40in / 97–101cm	CHEST (yd / m) 42–44in / 107–112cm	CHEST (yd / m) 46–48in / 117–122cm	WRAPS PER INCH
8 ply	10 / 6–7mm	170–275 / 155–250	16–18 and 22–23	1,300 / 1,190	1,600 / 1,460	1,900 / 1,740	2,200 / 2,010	24–26
10 ply	10 / 6–7mm	155–170 / 140–155	16–17 and 21–22	1,200 / 1,100	1,500 / 1,370	1,800 / 1,650	2,100 / 1,920	22–24

8-ply 100% nylon on 7 / 4.5mm needles in stockinette / stocking stitch

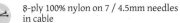 8-ply 100% nylon on 7 / 4.5mm needles in cable

8-ply 100% nylon on 7 / 4.5mm needles in lace

BULKY NYLON

Nylon in Bulky-weight yarn is quite light, so what it lacks in warmth it compensates for in volume. It is great for making quick, fun projects, but can be difficult to knit with if spun with feathery fibres. You can see in the swatches below, that with textured nylon blends, some stitch definition is lost.

GAUGE AND YARDAGE GUIDE

WEIGHT	RECOMMENDED NEEDLE SIZE	YARDAGE PER 100g (yd / m)	GAUGE / TENSION (stitches and rows per 4in / 10cm)	CHEST (yd / m) 34–36in / 86–91cm	CHEST (yd / m) 38–40in / 97–101cm	CHEST (yd / m) 42–44in / 107–112cm	CHEST (yd / m) 46–48in / 117–122cm	WRAPS PER INCH
12 ply	9–10¹/₂ / 5.5–6.5mm	110–150 / 100–140	14–16 and 18–20	1,100 / 1,005	1,400 / 1,280	1,700 / 1,560	2,000 / 1,830	18–20
14 ply	13 / 9mm	60–90 / 55–80	8–10 and 16–17	900 / 830	1,200 / 1,100	1,500 / 1,370	1,800 / 1,650	15–16

12-ply 50% nylon, 50% acrylic on 10¹/₂–11 / 7mm needles in stockinette / stocking stitch

12-ply 50% nylon, 50% acrylic on 10¹/₂–11 / 7mm needles in cable

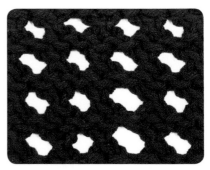

12-ply 50% nylon, 50% acrylic on 10¹/₂–11 / 7mm needles in lace

POLYESTER

Polyester, like nylon and acrylic, is derived from petroleum-based thermoplastics, and is also manufactured by a heat-bonding, filament-extrusion and melt-spin process. It is the manufacturers' secret formulas and additives that distinguish each of these synthetic fibres in appearance and character.

Polyester is a light, high-performance fibre that is crease- and shrink-resistant. As a pure yarn, it is spun in a wide variety of novelty yarns including feather, moiré and tape. It comes in many finishes, from spongy and textured to shiny and slinky. Polyester also blends well with natural fibres to create easy-care yarns. Novelty fibres can be knitted in several gauges; for example, a feathery polyester yarn can be knitted on very small needles for a full fur effect, or on large needles for a more open, airy knit. Because these yarns are fairly textured, they are best knitted with plain stitches. They make great accessories and garments, such as evening scarves and wraps, a fancy twin set, or children's fun knits and accessories.

SPECS

Source: Petroleum

Relative cost: An inexpensive fibre

Range of weights: 4 ply to 14 ply

Range of colours: Diverse range of pastels and muted tones to bright hues

USE AND CARE

Washing: Machine-washable

Drying: Machine-dryable

Notes: Cool iron

GENERAL QUALITIES

Look: Varied; can be light and spongy, smooth and shiny, or textured

Stitch definition: Low

Draping: Good

Pilling: Low

Resilience: Low elasticity

Durability: Good

Colour retention: High dye absorption

Feel: Can be spongy or slinky; slightly coarse against the skin

Warmth: Warm and light

Breathability: Low and conducts heat away from the body

Moisture resistance: Good wicking properties and dries quickly

Moisture wicking: Absorbs moisture readily

Allergens and toxins: Low allergy risk

Fire retardancy: Low flammability

Sustainability: A heavily manufactured fibre made from a finite resource; creates a great deal of environmental pollution and is not sustainable. However, there are some recycled polyester products on the market that offer a more eco-friendly option

POLYESTER BLENDS

Polyester is often blended with other natural fibres to create more easy-care garments and enhance durability and performance.

POLYESTER AND COTTON

Polyester is mixed with cotton to add shrink- and stain-resistance to this blend. Cotton makes the yarn more absorbent and comfortable.

SPECS

Relative cost: An inexpensive blend

Range of weights: 5 ply to 8 ply

Range of colours: Pastel and muted light tones, to bright and jewel colours

USE AND CARE

Washing: The addition of polyester makes this fibre mix machine-washable

Drying: Machine-dryable

Notes: Warm iron

QUICK TIPS

Try knitting feathery and moiré polyester yarns with larger needles than suggested, as the fluff fills the extra space around the stitches.

Textured polyester yarns are most suited to plain knitted stitches to best reveal the yarn's design.

GENERAL QUALITIES

Look: Smooth and shiny

Stitch definition: High

Draping: Good

Pilling: The presence of polyester in this blend reduces pilling

Resilience: Low elasticity

Durability: Polyester improves durability

Colour retention: Good

Feel: Soft and comfortable against the skin

Warmth: Polyester adds warmth

Breathability: Good

Moisture resistance: Moderate with the addition of cotton, which tends to absorb moisture readily

Moisture wicking: High moisture-absorption qualities

Allergens and toxins: Low allergenic mix

Fire retardancy: Polyester reduces flammability

Sustainability: Low

POLYESTER AND WOOL

Polyester is combined with wool to give it wrinkle-resistance and shape retention. The wool gives this blend good draping and elasticity.

SPECS

Relative cost: Less expensive than a pure wool blend

Range of weights: 8 ply to 12 ply

Range of colours: Muted and light pastels; earthy and dark colours

USE AND CARE

Washing: The addition of polyester makes this fibre mix machine-washable

Drying: Machine-washable at low temperatures

Notes: Avoid excess heat and agitation to prevent the wool from shrinking

PROS

- **Easy-care:**
  Polyester can be machine-washed and dried
- **Shrink-resistant:**
  Maintains shape and resists shrinkage
- **High-performance:**
  Can withstand climatic effects

CONS

- **Synthetic feel:**
  Polyester is a synthetic fibre and can feel static and brittle against the skin

GENERAL QUALITIES

Look: Shiny and textured

Stitch definition: Medium

Draping: Good

Pilling: Less pilling with the addition of polyester

Resilience: Good elasticity

Durability: Improved with the addition of polyester

Colour retention: Good

Feel: Soft against the skin

Warmth: Good

Breathability: Good

Moisture resistance: Good

Moisture wicking: Highly moisture-absorbent

Allergens and toxins: Polyester reduces the allergy risk of wool

Fire retardancy: Low flammability

Sustainability: Low

BURN TEST

Polyester shrinks away from flame and self-extinguishes.

POLYESTER WEIGHTS

FINE POLYESTER

Fine polyester is usually shiny or has a metallic look. It is great for making evening garments and accessories. Polyester is frequently used for novelty yarns, which are often very textured and/or colourful, both of which reduce stitch definition.

GAUGE AND YARDAGE GUIDE

WEIGHT	RECOMMENDED NEEDLE SIZE	YARDAGE PER 100g (yd / m)	GAUGE / TENSION (stitches and rows per 4in / 10cm)	CHEST (yd / m) 34–36in / 86–91cm	CHEST (yd / m) 38–40in / 97–101cm	CHEST (yd / m) 42–44in / 107–112cm	CHEST (yd / m) 46–48in / 117–122cm	WRAPS PER INCH
4–5 ply	8–9 / 5–5.5mm	500–600 / 460–550	20–24 and 26–28	1,600 / 1,460	1,800 / 1,650	2,100 / 1,920	2,400 / 2,195	18–22

4-ply 69% cotton, 31% polyester on 5 / 3.75mm needles in stockinette / stocking stitch

4-ply 69% cotton, 31% polyester on 5 / 3.75mm needles in cable

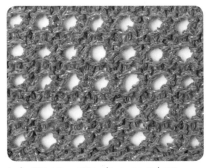

4-ply 69% cotton, 31% polyester on 5 / 3.75mm needles in lace

MEDIUM POLYESTER

Medium-weight polyester is often textured to produce a novelty yarn. It is a light yarn and suitable for making fancy and fun garments. Knitting on a small needle to favour the cable swatch, combined with the fuzzy texture of the yarn, has led to a very firm fabric with squashed stitches in the other two swatches.

GAUGE AND YARDAGE GUIDE

WEIGHT	RECOMMENDED NEEDLE SIZE	YARDAGE PER 100g (yd / m)	GAUGE / TENSION (stitches and rows per 4in / 10cm)	CHEST (yd / m) 34–36in / 86–91cm	CHEST (yd / m) 38–40in / 97–101cm	CHEST (yd / m) 42–44in / 107–112cm	CHEST (yd / m) 46–48in / 117–122cm	WRAPS PER INCH
8 ply	10 / 6–7mm	170–275 / 155–250	16–18 and 22–23	1,300 / 1,190	1,600 / 1,460	1,900 / 1,740	2,200 / 2,010	24–26
10 ply	10 / 6–7mm	155–170 / 140–155	16–17 and 21–22	1,200 / 1,100	1,500 / 1,370	1,800 / 1,650	2,100 / 1,920	22–24

8-ply 100% polyester on 8 / 5mm needles in stockinette / stocking stitch

8-ply 100% polyester on 8 / 5mm needles in cable

8-ply 100% polyester on 8 / 5mm needles in lace

BULKY POLYESTER

This novelty yarn is very light, but temperate, so makes great chunky jumpers and accessories without being too warm to wear.

GAUGE AND YARDAGE GUIDE

WEIGHT	RECOMMENDED NEEDLE SIZE	YARDAGE PER 100g (yd / m)	GAUGE / TENSION (stitches and rows per 4in / 10cm)	CHEST (yd / m) 34–36in / 86–91cm	CHEST (yd / m) 38–40in / 97–101cm	CHEST (yd / m) 42–44in / 107–112cm	CHEST (yd / m) 46–48in / 117–122cm	WRAPS PER INCH
12 ply	9–10½ / 5.5–6.5mm	110–150 / 100–140	10–12 and 14–16	1,100 / 1,005	1,400 / 1,280	1,700 / 1,560	2,000 / 1,830	10–12
14 ply	13 / 9mm	60–90 / 55–80	8–10 and 12–14	900 / 820	1,200 / 1,100	1,500 / 1,370	1,800 / 1,650	7–9

14-ply 100% polyester on 13 / 9mm needles in stockinette / stocking stitch

14-ply 100% polyester on 13 / 9mm needles in cable

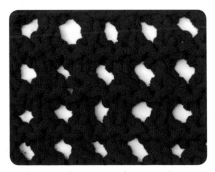

14-ply 100% polyester on 13 / 9mm needles in lace

ACRYLIC

Acrylic is a synthetic fibre made from petroleum products. It is regarded as a cheaper substitute for wool, while its twin fibre dralon is used as a substitute for cashmere. Acrylic is light, soft and warm, with good heat retention. Acrylic is often mixed with natural fibres to enhance the easy-care function, moth-resistance and light-fastness of a yarn. It is suitable for children's knits that need to be washed often, and is also a popular choice for socks. Acrylic is often included in novelty yarn mixes for textured effects in fashion yarns, and to add bulk and durability. These yarns are great for fun projects such as children's knits or teenagers' fashion knits.

SPECS

Source: Petroleum

Relative cost: An inexpensive fibre

Range of weights: 3 ply to 14 ply

Range of colours: Diverse range of pastels and muted tones to bright hues

USE AND CARE

Washing: Machine-washable

Drying: Dry jumpers flat; socks can be machine-dried

Notes: Cool iron

GENERAL QUALITIES

Look: Smooth with light brush

Stitch definition: Good

Draping: Good

Pilling: High pilling

Resilience: Good elasticity

Durability: Good

Colour retention: Low dye absorption but good colour-fastness

Feel: Soft and warm, but not as luxurious as natural fibres

Warmth: Warm and light

Breathability: Low

Moisture resistance: Good

Moisture wicking: Good moisture-carrying qualities but low absorption

Allergens and toxins: Can irritate sensitive skin

Fire retardancy: High flammability

Sustainability: A heavily processed fibre from a finite source, creating a great deal of environmental pollution

ACRYLIC AND NYLON

Acrylic and nylon blends create great easy-care yarns with good drape and memory. They are perfect for children's knits that need to be washed regularly. Acrylic and nylon also make a popular blend for sock yarn.

SPECS

Relative cost: An inexpensive yarn blend

Range of weights: 4 ply to 12 ply

Range of colours: Muted and light pastels; earthy and dark colours

USE AND CARE

Washing: Machine-washable

Drying: Machine-dryable

Notes: Extremely light-fast, so can be hung out in the sun

GENERAL QUALITIES

Look: Smooth with low sheen

Stitch definition: Good

Draping: Good

Pilling: Prone to pilling from the acrylic

Resilience: Good elasticity from the nylon

Durability: Good

Colour retention: Good colour retention and colour-fastness

Feel: Soft against the skin

Warmth: Good

Breathability: Low

Moisture resistance: Good

Moisture wicking: Highly moisture-absorbent

Allergens and toxins: Acrylic can be a skin irritant, but this is balanced with nylon, which has a low allergy risk

Fire retardancy: High flammability

Sustainability: Poor

ACRYLIC WEIGHTS

FINE ACRYLIC

Fine acrylic yarn is available on its own or blended with a natural fibre, such as wool, or with nylon for easy-care, economical yarns. This weight is perfect for babies' knits.

GAUGE AND YARDAGE GUIDE

WEIGHT	RECOMMENDED NEEDLE SIZE	YARDAGE PER 100g (yd / m)	GAUGE / TENSION (stitches and rows per 4in / 10cm)	CHEST (yd / m) 34–36in / 86–91cm	CHEST (yd / m) 38–40in / 97–101cm	CHEST (yd / m) 42–44in / 107–112cm	CHEST (yd / m) 46–48in / 117–122cm	WRAPS PER INCH
3 ply	1–3 / 2.25–3.25mm	500–600 / 460–550	30–32 and 34–35	1,600 / 1,460	1,900 / 1,740	2,200 / 2,010	2,500 / 2,290	25–27
4 ply	3 / 3.25mm	430–500 / 390–460	28–30 and 30–32	1,500 / 1,370	1,800 / 1,650	2,100 / 1,920	2,400 / 2,195	23–24
5 ply	3–4 / 3.25–3.5mm	400–420 / 365–385	24–26 and 28–29	1,400 / 1,280	1,700 / 1,560	2,000 / 1,830	2,300 / 2,100	21–22

4-ply 50% nylon, 50% acrylic on 2–3 / 3mm needles in stockinette / stocking stitch

4-ply 50% nylon, 50% acrylic on 2–3 / 3mm needles in cable

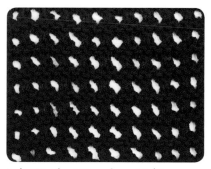

4-ply 50% nylon, 50% acrylic on 2–3 / 3mm needles in lace

MEDIUM ACRYLIC

Medium-weight acrylic yarn is a good weight for children's knits and colourwork. It is a light and lofty yarn in this weight. It is also blended with a variety of other fibres for novelty and fashion yarns, perfect for fun projects.

GAUGE AND YARDAGE GUIDE

WEIGHT	RECOMMENDED NEEDLE SIZE	YARDAGE PER 100g (yd / m)	GAUGE / TENSION (stitches and rows per 4in / 10cm)	CHEST (yd / m) 34–36in / 86–91cm	CHEST (yd / m) 38–40in / 97–101cm	CHEST (yd / m) 42–44in / 107–112cm	CHEST (yd / m) 46–48in / 117–122cm	WRAPS PER INCH
8 ply	5–6 / 3.75–4mm	350–380 / 320–350	20–24 and 25–27	1,300 / 1,190	1,600 / 1,460	1,900 / 1,740	2,200 / 2,010	19–20
10 ply	8–9 / 5–5.5mm	200–300 / 185–275	18–20 and 22–23	1,200 / 1,100	1,500 / 1370	1,800 / 1,650	2,100 / 1,920	15–18

8-ply 50% nylon, 50% acrylic on 7 / 4.5mm needles in stockinette / stocking stitch

8-ply 50% nylon, 50% acrylic on 7 / 4.5mm needles in cable

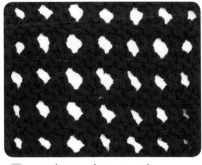

8-ply 50% nylon, 50% acrylic on 7 / 4.5mm needles in lace

BULKY ACRYLIC

Bulky acrylic is generally available as a mixed fibre blend for fashion yarns. It is a great choice for durable accessories, homewares and soft furnishings. It is also a good choice for making knitted toys.

GAUGE AND YARDAGE GUIDE

WEIGHT	RECOMMENDED NEEDLE SIZE	YARDAGE PER 100g (yd / m)	GAUGE / TENSION (stitches and rows per 4in / 10cm)	CHEST (yd / m) 34–36in / 86–91cm	CHEST (yd / m) 38–40in / 97–101cm	CHEST (yd / m) 42–44in / 107–112cm	CHEST (yd / m) 46–48in / 117–122cm	WRAPS PER INCH
12 ply	10–10½ / 6–6.5mm	140–180 / 130–165	14–16 and 18–20	1,100 / 1,005	1,400 / 1,280	1,700 / 1,560	2,000 / 1,830	10–12
14 ply	13–15 / 9–10mm	60–90 / 55–80	10–12 and 14–16	900 / 820	1,200 / 1,100	1,500 / 1,370	1,800 / 1,650	5–8

12 ply 52% wool, 34% acrylic, 14% polyamide on 10½ / 6.5mm needles in stockinette / stocking stitch

12-ply 52% wool, 34% acrylic, 14% polyamide on 10½ / 6.5mm needles in cable

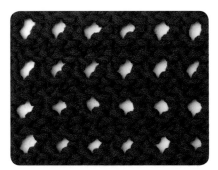

12-ply 52% wool, 34% acrylic, 14% polyamide on 10½ / 6.5mm needles in lace

BOUCLÉ

Bouclé has a loopy or curly character. It has an uneven look, as it is spun with at least two or more strands, one wound tighter than the other(s). The loose strand puffs out to create the loop. It is generally a fluffy yarn and is a great textural choice for a natural fibre blend. It is slower to knit with than a standard ply; you can try using smooth metal knitting needles to help with this. Always buy more bouclé yarn than you think you need, as it tends to scrunch up when knitted. Bouclé also comes in a variety of synthetic fibre blends as tonal, nubbly yarns.

SPECS

Source: Refer to specific yarn entries

Relative cost: Can be more expensive than a standard plied yarn

Range of weights: 2 ply to 10 ply

Range of colours: Broad: natural fibres range from light pastels to muted earthy tones and deep winter shades; synthetic colours are available in brilliant brights

USE AND CARE

Washing: Some bouclé yarns can shrink excessively when washed

Drying: Dry flat

Notes: Clean in a garment bag to avoid snags; brush lightly to re-fluff a garment

GENERAL QUALITIES

Look: Nubbly and loopy

Stitch definition: Low

Draping: Low to medium

Pilling: Low

Resilience: Bouclé gives yarn a high bounce with a curly twist

Durability: High; this twist strengthens the yarn

Colour retention: Refer to specific yarn entries

Feel: A bouclé twist can be rougher on the skin than a smooth, plied yarn

Warmth: Bouclé yarns are warm yet light, with added loft

Breathability: High

Moisture resistance: Refer to specific yarn entries

Moisture wicking: Bouclé is designed to be textured and lofty. This can create moisture-wicking properties in the fabric structure

Allergens and toxins: Refer to specific yarn entries

Fire retardancy: Depends on fibre content; refer to specific yarn entries

Sustainability: Depends on the fibre content, but novelty yarns tend to use more energy in their production so are less sustainable than natural-fibre yarns

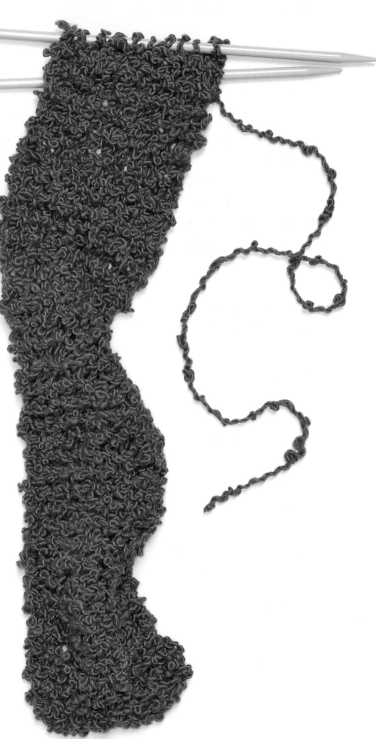

PROS

✂ **Easy to knit:**
Requires only simple knit stitches to show off the essence of the yarn

✂ **Springy:**
A bouclé spin adds springiness and high loft to inelastic fibres

✂ **Separation:**
A bouclé benefits 'sticky' yarns such as mohair by creating a separation in the yarn

CONS

✂ **Twist:**
As a multi-twist yarn, bouclé tends to tangle, knot and weaken during knitting

BOUCLÉ BLENDS

Bouclé yarns come in a vast array of pure fibres and blends. Fibres without elasticity and texture benefit from a bouclé spin, as this adds springiness and nubbly surface effects. Fibres with existing texture and fluff become even more snuggly when manufactured as a bouclé yarn. Synthetic bouclé mixes are an economical choice to create an organic and natural look.

BOUCLÉ: MOHAIR

Mohair fibre has a natural curl and spins beautifully as a bouclé yarn. It is often available handspun, as its characteristic looping reduces the time required for spinning. This yarn is perfect in a Bulky weight as it maintains the fibre's lightness and airiness, making it warm and comfortable to wear. Fine bouclé mohair is delicate, but not as sticky to knit with as a brushed, plied mohair.

SPECS

Relative cost: A bouclé mohair is more expensive than a plied mohair

Range of weights: 2 ply to 8 ply

Range of colours: Muted and soft pastels to bright hues and deep earthy tones

USE AND CARE

Washing: Wash on gentle machine cycle or handwash

Drying: Lay flat to dry

Notes: Can be dry-cleaned; lightly brush or shake garment dry to re-fluff

GENERAL QUALITIES

Look: Fluffy and nubbly

Stitch definition: Low

Draping: Medium; higher drape on fine knits

Pilling: Low

Resilience: There is a high spring action in a bouclé mohair

Durability: High

Colour retention: Mohair has good colour retention and the bouclé spin adds colour depth

Feel: Soft, however, the fuzzy texture can irritate the skin

Warmth: High

Breathability: The added loft of bouclé creates a breathable fabric

Moisture resistance: Mohair is moisture-resistant

Moisture wicking: High

Allergens and toxins: Low, although the fuzzy texture can irritate skin

Fire retardancy: High

Sustainability: High

BOUCLÉ: COTTON AND ACRYLIC OR NYLON

The blends of these fibres create all-season fabrics. The cotton is cool while the slub in bouclé adds cosiness, and the acrylic or nylon creates an elasticity that counters any over-drape in the cotton and adds springiness to close up the usual airiness of cotton knitting. Bouclé gives cotton, acrylic, and nylon a texture they lack naturally, but they maintain all their inherent softness and smoothness.

SPECS

Relative cost: This bouclé blend is inexpensive, but comparable to the same plied cotton blend

Range of weights: 5 ply to 10 ply

Range of colours: Variegated and mottled colour ranges

USE AND CARE

Washing: Machine-washable

Drying: Tumble dry at a low temperature

Notes: An easy-care yarn blend

GENERAL QUALITIES

Look: Loopy and rough

Stitch definition: Low

Draping: Medium

Pilling: Low

Resilience: Added spring from the bouclé is enhanced by the acrylic/nylon elasticity

Durability: High

Colour retention: Cotton will fade over time, while the acrylic and nylon will maintain their colour. Boucléd, all three will appear variegated over time

Feel: Knobbly against the skin, although soft and light

Warmth: The bouclé applied to these fibres makes for a warmer garment

Breathability: Cotton has superior breathability; nylon and acrylic have low breathability

Moisture resistance: High

Moisture wicking: There is less airflow through these fibres when boucléd than when plied; this reduces their otherwise high moisture-wicking qualities

Allergens and toxins: Low

Fire retardancy: Cotton and acrylic are highly flammable; nylon has a low flammability

Sustainability: Poor

QUICK TIP

Bouclé is rarely available as a Bulky-weight yarn, but can sometimes be found as an artisan handspun yarn.

BOUCLÉ WEIGHTS

FINE BOUCLÉ

Fine bouclé is soft and springy—ideal for fashion accessories. A larger needle is recommended than for other Fine yarns because the curls on a bouclé will fill out gaps in knitting. As stitch definition is poor with bouclé yarns, we have included only a stockinette / stocking stitch swatch here. Knitting a cable or lace stitch with a bouclé yarn would not give you a significantly different effect.

GAUGE AND YARDAGE GUIDE

WEIGHT	RECOMMENDED NEEDLE SIZE	YARDAGE PER 100g (yd / m)	GAUGE / TENSION (stitches and rows per 4in / 10cm)	CHEST (yd / m) 34–36in / 86–91cm	CHEST (yd / m) 38–40in / 97–101cm	CHEST (yd / m) 42–44in / 107–112cm	CHEST (yd / m) 46–48in / 117–122cm	WRAPS PER INCH
2 ply	6–7 / 4–4.5mm	380–400 / 350–365	26–28 and 28–30	1,700 / 1,560	2,000 / 1,830	2,300 / 2,105	2,600 / 2,380	40–42
3 ply	8–9 / 5–5.5mm	300–350 / 275–320	20–24 and 25–26	1,600 / 1,465	1,900 / 1,740	2,200 / 2,010	2,500 / 2,290	36–38
4–5 ply	9–10 / 5.5–6mm	200–250 / 180–230	16–18 and 23–24	1,500 / 1,370	1,800 / 1,650	2,100 / 1,920	2,400 / 2,200	36–38

2-ply 100% mohair on 6 / 4mm needles
in stockinette / stocking stitch

MEDIUM BOUCLÉ

Medium-weight bouclé is a comfortable weight for knitting and creates a dense fabric. It is a good yarn for making warm garments, but does not give good stitch definition. For this reason we have included only a stockinette / stocking stitch swatch here. Knitting a cable or lace stitch with a bouclé yarn would not give you a significantly different effect.

GAUGE AND YARDAGE GUIDE

WEIGHT	RECOMMENDED NEEDLE SIZE	YARDAGE PER 100g (yd / m)	GAUGE / TENSION (stitches and rows per 4in / 10cm)	CHEST (yd / m) 34–36in / 86–91cm	CHEST (yd / m) 38–40in / 97–101cm	CHEST (yd / m) 42–44in / 107–112cm	CHEST (yd / m) 46–48in / 117–122cm	WRAPS PER INCH
8 ply	10–11 / 6–8mm	150–180 / 140–165	12–14 and 21–22	1,400 / 1,280	1,700 / 1,560	2,000 / 1,830	2,300 / 2,100	26–28
10 ply	10–13 / 6–9mm	100–140 / 90–130	10–12 and 18–20	1,300 / 1,190	1,600 / 1,465	1,900 / 1,740	2,200 / 2,010	22–24

8-ply 100% alpaca on 10¹/₂–11 / 7mm needles
in stockinette / stocking stitch

CHENILLE

Chenille is a tufty, deep-pile yarn with fluffy, velvety texture. It is made using a coiled spinning process in which vertical tufts are anchored to a central core yarn. It is soft and lofty, with a bulky appearance that is iridescent due to the way the surface texture catches light. It can be manufactured from natural fibres such as cotton, wool and silk, or synthetic fibres such as acrylic and rayon. It can be difficult to work with, as it tends to worm while knitting, but with a few tricks this can be overcome. It is great in plain knitted stitches, as a jacquard pattern or in textured knitting featuring cables, bobbles or ripple stitches. It is moisture-absorbent because of its pile surface, so makes great bath towels and washcloths. It is also a good yarn for children's knits, blankets, baby clothes and accessories.

SPECS

Source: Refer to specific yarn entries

Relative cost: Can be more expensive than a standard plied yarn

Range of weights: 8 ply to 14 ply

Range of colours: From light pastels to muted earthy tones and deep winter shades; also brilliant brights

USE AND CARE

Washing: Some chenille yarns are machine-washable

Drying: Dry flat to avoid a heavy knit losing its shape

Notes: Do not iron

GENERAL QUALITIES

Look: Brushed and velvety

Stitch definition: Low

Draping: Medium

Pilling: Low

Resilience: High elasticity and good memory function

Durability: High; the twist strengthens the yarn

Colour retention: Refer to specific yarn entries

Feel: Soft against the skin

Warmth: Warm yet lighter with added loft

Breathability: Refer to specific yarn entries

Moisture resistance: High; pile is highly moisture-absorbent

Moisture wicking: Chenille is designed to be textured and lofty; this can create moisture-wicking properties in the fabric structure

Allergens and toxins: Refer to specific yarn entries

Fire retardancy: Depends on fibre content; refer to specific yarn entries

Sustainability: Depends on the fibre content, but synthetic yarns tend to use more energy in their production so are less sustainable than natural fibres

PROS

🖊 Velvety:
Chenille adds texture to a project without additional fluff and the fibre shedding common with novelty yarns

🖊 Springy:
A chenille spin adds springiness, bulk, and loft to knitted garments

CONS

🖊 Worming:
As a high-twist yarn, chenille tends to worm when knitting (worming is when the yarn detaches from the knitting and coils back on itself)

CHENILLE BLENDS

Chenille yarns come in a vast array of pure fibres and blends, but they are not generally available as Fine-weight yarns. Fibres without loft, such as cotton, rayon, and silk benefit from a chenille spin, as it adds three-dimensional qualities with surface texture.

CHENILLE: COTTON

Cotton chenille is soft and plush and has less tendency to worm like other chenille fibres. Cotton benefits from a chenille spin, as it adds texture and springiness to this yarn.

SPECS

Relative cost: Cotton chenille is more expensive than plied cotton

Range of weights: 8 ply to 12 ply

Range of colours: Soft pastels to bright hues

USE AND CARE

Washing: Cotton yarn can be machine-washed

Drying: Dry flat to avoid warping

Notes: Iron on the reverse of a garment, as the surface will reflect the iron imprint

GENERAL QUALITIES

Look: Brushed and velvety

Stitch definition: Low

Draping: Medium

Pilling: Prone to pilling

Resilience: A chenille texture adds springiness to cotton

Durability: High

Colour retention: Cotton fades over time

Feel: Soft and cool

Warmth: Moderate; chenille improves warmth as it adds bulk

Breathability: The added loft of chenille improves the breathability of the fabric

Moisture resistance: High

Moisture wicking: Cotton chenille has good moisture absorption

Allergens and toxins: Low

Fire retardancy: High

Sustainability: A cotton chenille yarn is highly processed, using a lot of energy. It is not environmentally sustainable, particularly if the cotton is not organically grown

CHENILLE: POLYESTER

Polyester chenille is popular as a cheaper alternative to cotton chenille. It is warmer, and has a slightly spongier appearance than velvety cotton chenille, but it still has a soft, lofty feel. It is also referred to as polar yarn. Polyester makes the yarn easy-care, which means that knitted garments can be machine-washed and -dried. This blend is a good choice for babies' and children's knits.

SPECS

Relative cost: An inexpensive blend

Range of weights: 8 ply to 14 ply

Range of colours: Pastels to brights, and dark winter colours

QUICK TIPS

Worming is problematic with chenille. Here are a couple of tips to overcome this:

- Use smaller needles than recommended to keep knitting firm, as this will lessen its tendency to worm.

- Knit from the other end of the yarn so the twist you introduce is in reverse to the yarn's own twist.

USE AND CARE

Washing: This yarn blend is machine-washable

Drying: Tumble dry at a low temperature

Notes: An easy-care yarn blend

GENERAL QUALITIES

Look: Brushed, matte and rubbery

Stitch definition: Low

Draping: Medium

Pilling: Low

Resilience: High elasticity

Durability: High

Colour retention: High

Feel: Soft

Warmth: Warm and light

Breathability: Breathes well and conducts heat away from the body

Moisture resistance: High

Moisture wicking: High

Allergens and toxins: Low

Fire retardancy: Low flammability

Sustainability: Low

CHENILLE WEIGHTS

MEDIUM CHENILLE

Medium-weight chenille is a comfortable weight for knitting and creates a light yet warm fabric for children's or babies' knits.

GAUGE AND YARDAGE GUIDE

WEIGHT	RECOMMENDED NEEDLE SIZE	YARDAGE PER 100g (yd / m)	GAUGE / TENSION (wrap and rows per 4in / 10cm)	CHEST (yd / m) 34–36in / 86–91cm	CHEST (yd / m) 38–40in / 97–101cm	CHEST (yd / m) 42–44in / 107–112cm	CHEST (yd / m) 46–48in / 117–122cm	WRAPS PER INCH
8 ply	6–8 / 4–5mm	150–200 / 140–180	16–18 and 18–20	1,310 / 1,200	1,485 / 1,360	1,660 / 1,520	1,835 / 1,680	12–14
10 ply	8–9 / 5–5.5mm	120–140 / 110–130	13–14 and 16–18	1,200 / 1,100	1,375 / 1,260	1,550 / 1,420	1,725 / 1,580	10–12

8-ply 100% cotton chenille on 6 / 4mm needles in stockinette / stocking stitch

8-ply 100% cotton chenille on 6 / 4mm needles in cable

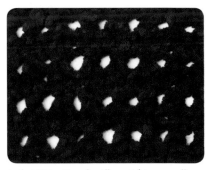

8-ply 100% cotton chenille on 6 / 4mm needles in lace

BULKY CHENILLE

Chenille in a Bulky weight is a popular yarn. It is great for making quick, chunky accessories and children's projects. When knitted with bigger needles, it creates a breathable fabric with a good balance of warmth and comfort.

GAUGE AND YARDAGE GUIDE

WEIGHT	RECOMMENDED NEEDLE SIZE	YARDAGE PER 100g (yd / m)	GAUGE / TENSION (stitches and rows per 4in / 10cm)	CHEST (yd / m) 34–36in / 86–91cm	CHEST (yd / m) 38–40in / 97–101cm	CHEST (yd / m) 42–44in / 107–112cm	CHEST (yd / m) 46–48in / 117–122cm	WRAPS PER INCH
12 ply	11 / 8mm	50–110 / 45–100	8–12 and 14–16	1,120 / 1,020	1,295 / 1,180	1,470 / 1,340	1,645 / 1,500	8–9
14 ply	17 / 12.5mm	20–30 / 18–27	4–6 and 10–12	1,100 / 1,000	1,275 / 1,160	1,450 / 1,320	1,625 / 1,480	6–8

14-ply 100% polyester on 15 / 12mm needles in stockinette / stocking stitch

14-ply 100% polyester on 15 / 12mm needles in cable

14-ply 100% polyester on 15 / 12mm needles in lace

RIBBON

Ribbon yarns come in a range of knitted tapes that can be tubular, flat, mesh, curly, crimped, ruffled or bias. They can be made from a range of natural fibres including silk, cotton, tencel and wool, and synthetic fibres such as nylon, rayon, polyester and acrylic. Ribbon yarns have a myriad of finishes with dyed colours knitted or woven into the tape, in contrasting, marbled, variegated and striped colour effects. Some ribbon yarns are silky, some matte, brushed and airy, and some have faux suede or leather looks. Woven tape yarns are quite inelastic, unless blended with elastic fibres such as wool or nylon. Because of their tape structure, ribbon yarns knit up as Medium- or Bulky-weight fabrics and have a three-dimensional look when knitted. Ribbon yarn is a good choice for making eye-catching accessories or fancy trims.

SPECS

Source: Refer to specific yarn entries

Relative cost: Can be more expensive than a standard plied yarn

Range of weights: 8 ply to 12 ply

Range of colours: From light pastels and muted leather tones to brilliant mixed brights

USE AND CARE

Washing: Will depend on fibre content

Drying: Will depend on fibre content

Notes: Refer to specific yarn entries

GENERAL QUALITIES

Look: Varies from suede-like to shiny and slinky

Stitch definition: Low

Draping: Medium

Pilling: Low

Resilience: Low elasticity

Durability: High

Colour retention: Refer to specific yarn entries

Feel: Refer to specific yarn entries

Warmth: Refer to specific yarn entries

Breathability: Refer to specific yarn entries

Moisture resistance: Refer to specific yarn entries

Moisture wicking: Refer to specific yarn entries

Allergens and toxins: Refer to specific yarn entries

Fire retardancy: Depends on fibre content; refer to specific yarn entries

Sustainability: Depends on the fibre content, but synthetic novelty yarns tend to use more energy in their production than natural fibres so are less sustainable

PROS

✁ **Colour:**
Ribbon tape yarns come in an enormous variety of colours and finishes

CONS

✁ **Slippery:**
Fibres such as silk, polyester and acrylic tape yarns tend to slip, twist and de-ball very easily during knitting

QUICK TIP

Try using bamboo needles to reduce slippage while working with slinky tape yarns.

RIBBON BLENDS

Inelastic fibres woven or knitted into ribbon yarns are usually mixed with nylon or wool to create elasticity in the blend. Fibres are also added to create a more economical yarn blend such as acrylic mixed with wool or silk.

RIBBON: SILK

Ribbon silk is a soft, luxurious and draping yarn to knit with. It is temperature-moderating, as the knit structure from the tape has excellent airflow, meaning that it can be cool in summer and warm in winter. For this reason it is a lovely yarn to use for inter-season fashions and accessories.

SPECS

Relative cost: Silk tape is an expensive yarn

Range of weights: 8 ply to 12 ply

Range of colours: Soft pastels to bright hues

USE AND CARE

Washing: Gentle handwash

Drying: Dry flat to avoid warping

Notes: Do not iron

GENERAL QUALITIES

Look: Lightly wrinkled with high sheen

Stitch definition: Medium

Draping: Good

Pilling: Low

Resilience: Good stretch and elasticity

Durability: High

Colour retention: Medium light-fastness

Feel: Soft and luxurious

Warmth: Moderate

Breathability: The added loft of the three-dimensional ribbon in knitted fabric improves the breathability

Moisture resistance: High

Moisture wicking: Ribbon silk has high moisture absorption

Allergens and toxins: Low

Fire retardancy: Low

Sustainability: Poor; ribbon silk yarn is highly processed and therefore energy-intensive

RIBBON: COTTON AND NYLON

Cotton and nylon ribbon yarn comes in a variety of looks from matte polar to shiny and colourful. Cotton benefits from the elasticity and drape of nylon, and the blend can be manufactured in a huge range of fancy finishes and textural effects. Cotton adds softness and breathability to the blend. This yarn is a good choice for children's knits and for special accessory projects, such as bags and jewellery.

SPECS

Relative cost: An inexpensive blend
Range of weights: 8 ply to 12 ply
Range of colours: Pastels to brights and dark colours

USE AND CARE

Washing: Machine-washable
Drying: Tumble dry at a low temperature
Notes: An easy-care yarn blend

GENERAL QUALITIES

Look: Mesh, matte and leathery
Stitch definition: Low
Draping: Medium
Pilling: Low
Resilience: Nylon improves elasticity
Durability: High
Colour retention: High
Feel: Soft
Warmth: Cool and light
Breathability: Breathes well and conducts heat away from the body
Moisture resistance: High
Moisture wicking: High
Allergens and toxins: Low
Fire retardancy: Low flammability
Sustainability: Low

RIBBON WEIGHTS

MEDIUM RIBBON

Medium-gauge ribbon is a comfortable weight for knitting and creates a bulky but light fabric for fancy accessories or jumpers. With such a highly textured yarn, stitch definition will always be poor.

GAUGE AND YARDAGE GUIDE

WEIGHT	RECOMMENDED NEEDLE SIZE	YARDAGE PER 100g (yd / m)	GAUGE / TENSION (stitches and rows per 4in / 10cm)	CHEST (yd / m) 34–36in / 86–91cm	CHEST (yd / m) 38–40in / 97–101cm	CHEST (yd / m) 42–44in / 107–112cm	CHEST (yd / m) 46–48in / 117–122cm	WRAPS PER INCH
8 ply	4–6 / 3.5–4mm	180–240 / 160–220	20–24 and 20–24	1,200 / 1,095	1,500 / 1,370	1,800 / 1,650	2,100 / 1,920	22–24
10 ply	8–9 / 5–5.5mm	140–160 / 130–146	16–18 and 18–20	1,100 / 1,010	1,400 / 1,280	1,700 / 1,560	2,000 / 1,830	20–22

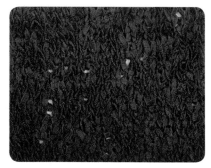

8-ply 100% silk on 7 / 4.5mm needles in stockinette / stocking stitch

8-ply 100% silk on 7 / 4.5mm needles in cable

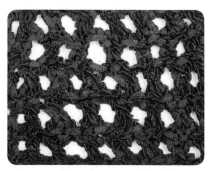

8-ply 100% silk on 7 / 4.5mm needles in lace

BULKY RIBBON

Bulky ribbon yarn is great for quick projects on big needles, and it creates a breathable, chunky fabric. It is perfect for accessories such as scarves, wraps or three-dimensional projects such as bags and hats.

GAUGE AND YARDAGE GUIDE

WEIGHT	RECOMMENDED NEEDLE SIZE	YARDAGE PER 100g (yd / m)	GAUGE / TENSION (stitches and rows per 4in / 10cm)	CHEST (yd / m) 34–36in / 86–91cm	CHEST (yd / m) 38–40in / 97–101cm	CHEST (yd / m) 42–44in / 107–112cm	CHEST (yd / m) 46–48in / 117–122cm	WRAPS PER INCH
12 ply	11 / 8mm	50–110 / 45–100	8–12 and 12–16	1,000 / 915	1,300 / 1,190	1,600 / 1,460	1,900 / 1,740	10–16

12 ply 45% nylon, 36% polyester, 19% cotton on 11 / 8mm needles in stockinette / stocking stitch

12-ply 45% nylon, 36% polyester, 19% cotton on 11 / 8mm needles in cable

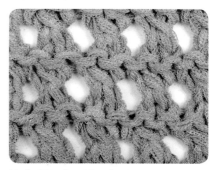

12-ply 45% nylon, 36% polyester, 19% cotton on 11 / 8mm needles in lace

EYELASH

Eyelash or feather yarns feature tufts of threads attached intermittently to a core yarn. The tufts can be long, short, uneven, straight or curly, and are mostly manufactured from polyester, or rayon and nylon mixes. These yarns are available in a wide range of colours and the finishes can be bright, metallic or faux fur. Eyelash yarn is a bold, warm yarn to work with, and knits up to a chunky fabric, with the tufts creating a fur-like effect on one side of the knitting. Short-tufted eyelash yarn is available in weights from 3 ply to 8 ply, while long-tufted yarns are available in Bulky weights from 10 ply to 14 ply. Eyelash yarn is a great choice for making unusual accessories or trims, or for fashion-forward garments.

SPECS

Source: Refer to specific yarn entries

Relative cost: Can be more expensive than a standard plied yarn

Range of weights: 5 ply to 14 ply

Range of colours: From light pastels to muted fur tones to brilliant mixed brights

USE AND CARE

Washing: Polyester eyelash fabrics can be machine-washed

Drying: Polyester eyelash fabrics can be machine-dried

Notes: Lightly shake the garment to fluff up the feathery effect

GENERAL QUALITIES

Look: Varies from feathery to furry effects

Stitch definition: Low

Draping: Medium

Pilling: Low

Resilience: Depends on core yarn content, but generally low to medium elasticity

Durability: High

Colour retention: Refer to specific yarn entries

Feel: Soft, although synthetic

Warmth: Good

Breathability: The aerated three-dimensional quality of this yarn when knitted up creates a good breathable fabric

Moisture resistance: Refer to specific yarn entries

Moisture wicking: Refer to specific yarn entries

Allergens and toxins: Polyester is a low irritant, but the feathery texture of the yarn may irritate skin

Fire retardancy: Depends on fibre content; refer to specific yarn entries

Sustainability: Depends on the fibre content, but novelty yarns tend to use a lot of energy in their production

PROS

✎ Colour:
Eyelash tape yarns come in an enormous variety of colours and finishes

CONS

✎ Poor stitch definition:
Eyelash yarns have poor stitch definition, which makes it difficult to see errors and count rows

EYELASH BLENDS

Eyelash yarns are predominantly 100% polyester. However, some are mixes of nylon and acrylic for the core thread, with the tufts or feathers being mixes of mohair, wool and other fibres. This adds elasticity to the yarn, along with durability and economy.

EYELASH: POLYESTER

Polyester can be adapted for many manufacturing processes and is popularly applied to eyelash yarns for a variety of looks. It is usually a long, feathery yarn and is ideal for fun knitting projects and creating fashion-forward looks for accessories and garments. It is an easy-care yarn.

SPECS

Relative cost: An inexpensive blend

Range of weights: 3 ply to 14 ply

Range of colours: Soft pastels to bright hues and faux-fur colours

USE AND CARE

Washing: Machine-washable

Drying: Machine-dryable

Notes: Do not iron; lightly fluff up surface nap

GENERAL QUALITIES

Look: Feathery and/or furry

Stitch definition: Low

Draping: Good

Pilling: Low

Resilience: There is a good spring to this yarn

Durability: High

Colour retention: High

Feel: Soft and furry

Warmth: Good warmth yet light

Breathability: The added loft of the three-dimensional eyelash yarn creates a breathable fabric

Moisture resistance: Good

Moisture wicking: Good

Allergens and toxins: Low, although the feathery fluff may irritate the skin

Fire retardancy: Low

Sustainability: Poor, as polyester eyelash yarn is highly processed and therefore energy-intensive

EYELASH: RAYON AND NYLON

Rayon and nylon mixed as an eyelash yarn usually has nylon as the core yarn for elasticity and rayon as the attached tufts for shine and sparkle. It is a good choice for making glamorous evening accessories such as shrugs, stoles or fancy wraps; or accessory projects such as bags and jewellery.

SPECS

Relative cost: An inexpensive blend

Range of weights: 5 ply to 14 ply

Range of colours: Pastels to bright jewel tones, and moody evening colours

USE AND CARE

Washing: Machine-washable

Drying: Tumble dry at a low temperature

Notes: An easy-care yarn blend

GENERAL QUALITIES

Look: Shiny and spidery or frothy

Stitch definition: Low

Draping: Good

Pilling: Low

Resilience: Nylon improves the elasticity of this blend

Durability: High

Colour retention: High

Feel: Soft

Warmth: Good warmth yet light

Breathability: Breathes well with the added loft of the yarn structure

Moisture resistance: High

Moisture wicking: High

Allergens and toxins: Low

Fire retardancy: Low flammability

Sustainability: Poor

QUICK TIP

Often an eyelash yarn's belly band will indicate its gauge as 'various'. This is because the thin-and-thick nature of the core yarn and the attached lash means it can be knitted up in a range of fabrics from fine to heavy.

EYELASH WEIGHTS

FINE EYELASH

Fine eyelash yarn has a very fine eyelash thread on a fine core yarn. However, it knits up with a slightly heavier appearance due to the extra dimension of the eyelash, even though it is a fine and softly draping fabric. This yarn weight will make lovely accessories. As stitch definition is so poor with eyelash yarns, we have included only a stockinette / stocking stitch swatch for this yarn. Knitting a cable or lace stitch with an eyelash yarn would not give you a significantly different effect.

GAUGE AND YARDAGE GUIDE

WEIGHT	RECOMMENDED NEEDLE SIZE	YARDAGE PER 100g (yd / m)	GAUGE / TENSION (stitches and rows per 4in / 10cm)	CHEST (yd / m) 34–36in / 86–91cm	CHEST (yd / m) 38–40in / 97–101cm	CHEST (yd / m) 42–44in / 107–112cm	CHEST (yd / m) 46–48in / 117–122cm	WRAPS PER INCH
3 ply	2–3 / 2.75–3.25mm	350–400 / 320–365	28–32 and 28–32	1,500 / 1,370	1,800 / 1,650	2,100 / 1,920	2,400 / 2,195	30–33
4–5 ply	3–8 / 3.25–5mm	300–400 / 275–365	25–27 and 22–24	1,400 / 1,280	1,700 / 1,550	2,000 / 1,830	2,300 / 2,000	22–24

5-ply 100% polyester on 6 / 4mm needles in stockinette / stocking stitch

QUICK TIP

Eyelash yarns are bulky when knitted. Knitting with bigger needles than suggested creates a cobweb look that is very flattering on the body, and will create a lovely drape for evening looks.

MEDIUM EYELASH

Medium eyelash yarns have short tufts and create a lovely fur-like effect when knitted up. They can be knitted in various gauges because of their thick-and-thin characteristic. On smaller needles they create a solid fur look; on larger needles, the fur will create a more open-weave effect. As stitch definition is so poor with eyelash yarns, we have included only a stockinette / stocking stitch swatch for this yarn. Knitting a cable or lace stitch with an eyelash yarn would not give you a significantly different effect.

GAUGE AND YARDAGE GUIDE

WEIGHT	RECOMMENDED NEEDLE SIZE	YARDAGE PER 100g (yd / m)	GAUGE / TENSION (stitches and rows per 4in / 10cm)	CHEST (yd / m) 34–36in / 86–91cm	CHEST (yd / m) 38–40in / 97–101cm	CHEST (yd / m) 42–44in / 107–112cm	CHEST (yd / m) 46–48in / 117–122cm	WRAPS PER INCH
8 ply	4–6 / 3.5–4mm	180–240 / 160–220	20–24 and 20–22	1,200 / 1,095	1,500 / 1,370	1,800 / 1,650	2,100 / 1,920	22–24
10 ply	8–9 / 5–5.5mm	140–160 / 130–146	16–18 and 18–19	1,100 / 1,020	1,400 / 1,280	1,700 / 1,560	2,000 / 1,830	19–21

8-ply 50% nylon, 50% polyester on 6 / 4mm
needles in lace

BULKY EYELASH

If knitted with a tight tension, this yarn will create a fur-like effect on one side. When knitted with bigger needles for an open knit, the fabric will have a more open, lacy look, which creates a flattering drape if used for garments. As stitch definition is so poor with eyelash yarns, we have included only a stockinette / stocking stitch swatch for this yarn. Knitting a cable or lace stitch with an eyelash yarn would not give you a significantly different effect.

GAUGE AND YARDAGE GUIDE

WEIGHT	RECOMMENDED NEEDLE SIZE	YARDAGE PER 100g (yd / m)	GAUGE / TENSION (stitches and rows per 4in / 10cm)	CHEST (yd / m) 34–36in / 86–91cm	CHEST (yd / m) 38–40in / 97–101cm	CHEST (yd / m) 42–44in / 107–112cm	CHEST (yd / m) 46–48in / 117–122cm	WRAPS PER INCH
12 ply	11 / 8mm	100–120 / 90–110	12–14 and 16–18	1,000 / 915	1,300 / 1,190	1,600 / 1,460	1,900 / 1,740	16–18
14 ply	13–17 / 9–15mm	70–90 / 65–80	10–12 and 14–16	900 / 820	1,200 / 1,100	1,500 / 1,370	1,800 / 1,650	14–16

12-ply 100% microfibre nylon on 8 / 5mm needles in stockinette / stocking stitch

FLAMME

Flamme yarn is a loosely plied thick-and-thin yarn. It has a core thread in a single roving, which is wrapped by a lightly twisted thread of thick-and-thin texture. With its rippled, slubby character, it resembles a hand-spun yarn. It is usually available in natural fibres (cotton, wool, silk and alpaca), in both pure blends and in mixes, making soft and luxurious yarns. It is a warm, Bulky-weight yarn, but very light and aerated due to its low twist. It creates a lovely textured fabric that can look good in garter stitch and cable patterns.

SPECS

Source: Refer to specific yarn entries

Relative cost: Can cost more than a standard plied yarn

Range of weights: 10 ply

Range of colours: Warm earthy tones

USE AND CARE

Washing: Natural-fibre flamme yarns require gentle handwashing with little agitation to avoid shrinkage

Drying: Dry flat to maintain shape

Notes: Cool iron or light steam so as to not flatten the surface

PROS

⚲ Texture:
Flamme yarns have a wonderful slubbiness usually only found in handspun yarns

⚲ Springiness:
A flamme yarn can add spring to inelastic yarns due to the airy buoyancy of the low-ply twist

CONS

⚲ Shrinkage:
Some cotton flamme yarns tend to shrink

GENERAL QUALITIES

Look: Slubby

Stitch definition: Medium

Draping: Good

Pilling: Refer to specific yarn entries

Resilience: Refer to specific yarn entries

Durability: A low-twist yarn tends to have weak spots

Colour retention: Refer to specific yarn entries

Feel: Soft

Warmth: Good

Breathability: The aerated, three-dimensional quality of this yarn when knitted up creates good breathability

Moisture resistance: Refer to specific yarn entries

Moisture wicking: Refer to specific yarn entries

Allergens and toxins: Refer to specific yarn entries

Fire retardancy: Depends on the fibre content; refer to specific yarn entries

Sustainability: Depends on the fibre content; refer to specific yarn entries

FLAMME BLENDS

Flamme yarns are available in silk and cotton pure or mixed blends, sometimes with wool and alpaca. Great yarns for the fibre enthusiast, they reveal the character of the fibre well. Their features bloom in this yarn spin, showcasing the natural fluffiness of cotton, the lustre of silk and alpaca, and the crimp of wool.

FLAMME: SILK, WOOL AND ALPACA

This is an enchanting blend. It has the warmth of alpaca, the versatile properties of wool and the elegance, sheen and drape of silk. It has a bulky appearance and good warmth. It can be used to make beautiful ponchos, hats, scarves and wraps, as well as jumpers and cardigans.

SPECS

Relative cost: An expensive yarn mix

Range of weights: 10 ply

Range of colours: Earthy, wintry tones

USE AND CARE

Washing: Gentle handwash with tepid water, avoiding excess agitation to prevent shrinkage

Drying: Dry flat

Notes: Cool iron

GENERAL QUALITIES

Look: Slubby

Stitch definition: Good

Draping: Good

Pilling: Prone to pilling

Resilience: There is a good spring and elasticity in this yarn

Durability: High

Colour retention: High

Feel: Soft and warm

Warmth: Good warmth yet quite light

Breathability: Good

Moisture resistance: Good

Moisture wicking: Good

Allergens and toxins: Wool and alpaca can cause allergic reactions with sensitive skin

Fire retardancy: Low

Sustainability: Moderately sustainable if the silk and wool production are ecologically responsible

FLAMME: COTTON

This yarn has a lovely slubby appearance and benefits from the natural softness and lightness of cotton. It is a Bulky-weight yarn, so is perfect for making chunky garments without too much warmth.

SPECS

Relative cost: More expensive than a standard plied cotton

Range of weights: 10 ply

Range of colours: Pastels to bright colours

USE AND CARE

Washing: Handwash to avoid too much shrinkage, as cotton yarns can tend to shrink

Drying: Dry flat

Notes: Dry-cleanable

GENERAL QUALITIES

Look: Slubby with light sheen

Stitch definition: Low

Draping: Good

Pilling: Low

Resilience: Improved slightly with the loftiness of the fibre

Durability: High

Colour retention: High, but fades over time

Feel: Soft

Warmth: Cool and light

Breathability: Improved with the added loft of the yarn

Moisture resistance: High

Moisture wicking: High

Allergens and toxins: Low

Fire retardancy: High

Sustainability: Poor

QUICK TIP

A wool flamme yarn is great for knitting and felting projects due to the loose-ply roving character of the yarn. Ensure the wool is not a superwash yarn if you want to use it for this purpose.

FLAMME WEIGHTS

BULKY FLAMME

Flamme yarns have a chunky character due to their thick-and-thin roving spin. Flamme is wonderful yarn to use for jumper projects and will knit up beautifully in plain garter and stocking stitch or in fancy textured and cable stitches.

GAUGE AND YARDAGE GUIDE

WEIGHT	RECOMMENDED NEEDLE SIZE	YARDAGE PER 100g (yd / m)	GAUGE / TENSION (stitches and rows per 4in / 10cm)	CHEST (yd / m) 34–36in / 86–91cm	CHEST (yd / m) 38–40in / 97–101cm	CHEST (yd / m) 42–44in / 107–112cm	CHEST (yd / m) 46–48in / 117–122cm	WRAPS PER INCH
10 ply	10 / 6mm	150–170 / 140–155	14–16 and 20–23	1,100 / 1,005	1,400 / 1,280	1,700 / 1,560	2,000 / 1,830	12

10-ply 50% Peruvian wool, 30% alpaca, 20% silk on 10½–11 / 7mm needles in stockinette / stocking stitch

10-ply 50% Peruvian wool, 30% alpaca, 20% silk on 10½–11 / 7mm needles in cable

10-ply 50% Peruvian wool, 30% alpaca, 20% silk on 10½–11 / 7mm needles in lace

LADDER

Ladder yarn is ribbon yarn that resembles a ladder, with two parallel threads connected by an intermittently spaced strip of fibre in the middle. The threads on the outside resemble a cord that is fine and firm, while the middle fibres are soft and can be meshed, metallic or tufted and fluffy. Sometimes beads and sequins are added for fancy evening looks. Ladder yarns usually have a lightweight and lacy structure. They are often produced in nylon for a summer-weight yarn. Ladder yarns come in a variety of colour ranges and effects, from multicolour and shiny to matte, soft and subtle shades. They come in Medium- to Bulky-weight yarns; due to the extra bulk from the width of the tape, ladder yarn is not generally available in Fine weights. Ladder yarns can be knitted firmly to make trims, headbands and jewellery, or knitted loosely on big needles to create cobwebby scarves, shawls, wraps and singlets.

SPECS

Source: Refer to specific yarn entries

Relative cost: Can cost more than a standard plied yarn

Range of weights: 8 ply to 12 ply

Range of colours: Bright jewel and multicolour mixes, to soft, subtle, muted and pastel shades

USE AND CARE

Washing: Gentle handwash to avoid snags and pulls

Drying: Dry flat to maintain shape

Notes: Do not iron

GENERAL QUALITIES

Look: Lacy

Stitch definition: Low

Draping: Good

Pilling: Refer to specific yarn entries

Resilience: Some ladder yarn mixes have nylon for elasticity; otherwise it is a fairly inelastic yarn

Durability: Good

Colour retention: Refer to specific yarn entries

Feel: Soft and cool

Warmth: Low

Breathability: The three-dimensional quality of this yarn creates good breathability

Moisture resistance: Refer to specific yarn entries

Moisture wicking: Refer to specific yarn entries

Allergens and toxins: Refer to specific yarn entries

Fire retardancy: Depends on the fibre content; refer to specific yarn entries

Sustainability: Depends on the fibre content; refer to specific yarn entries

PROS

- **Texture:**
  Creates wonderful drape and lacy cobweb effects with open knitting
- **Drape:**
  Has a lovely draping quality

CONS

- **Snags:**
  Open-work lace knitting can cause snags when wearing and washing

LADDER BLENDS

Ladder yarn is commonly available in nylon for an elastic yarn with a shiny finish. It is sometimes mixed with lurex or acrylic to create sparkly yarns. Sometimes another yarn is threaded through the ladder to create a different look.

LADDER: NYLON

This is a soft, lightweight, lacy yarn that comes in a variety of ribbon widths to create Fine-, Medium-, and Bulky-weight yarns. It is a lovely yarn to make unusual scarves, shawls, ponchos and wraps.

SPECS

Relative cost: An inexpensive yarn mix

Range of weights: 8 ply to 12 ply

Range of colours: Bright and rainbow colours to muted soft pastels and dark earthy colours

USE AND CARE

Washing: Gentle handwash to avoid snags and pulls

Drying: Dry flat to maintain shape

Notes: Cool iron

GENERAL QUALITIES

Look: Meshy and lacy

Stitch definition: Low

Draping: Good

Pilling: Low

Resilience: Good springiness and elasticity

Durability: High

Colour retention: High

Feel: Cool and light

Warmth: Moderate

Breathability: Good

Moisture resistance: Good

Moisture wicking: Good

Allergens and toxins: Low allergy risk

Fire retardancy: Low

Sustainability: Poor

LADDER: NYLON AND LUREX

This yarn has an eye-catching sparkly finish, and is perfect for making glamorous evening knits.

SPECS

Relative cost: More expensive than a standard plied nylon

Range of weights: 8 ply

Range of colours: Bright colours

USE AND CARE

Washing: Gentle handwash to avoid snags and pulls

Drying: Dry flat to maintain shape

Notes: Do not iron

GENERAL QUALITIES

Look: Sparkly and lacy

Stitch definition: Low

Draping: Good

Pilling: Low

Resilience: Good springiness and elasticity

Durability: High

Colour retention: High

Feel: Cool and light

Warmth: Moderate

Breathability: Good

Moisture resistance: Good

Moisture wicking: Good

Allergens and toxins: Low allergy risk

Fire retardancy: Low

Sustainability: Poor

LADDER WEIGHTS

MEDIUM LADDER

Medium ladder yarns can be knitted up with bigger needles than suggested to create a drapey, cobwebby effect for wraps, shawls and ponchos. As stitch definition is so poor with ladder yarns, we have included only a stockinette / stocking stitch swatch for this yarn. Knitting a cable or lace stitch with a ladder yarn would not give you a significantly different effect.

GAUGE AND YARDAGE GUIDE

WEIGHT	RECOMMENDED NEEDLE SIZE	YARDAGE PER 100g (yd / m)	GAUGE / TENSION (stitches and rows per 4in / 10cm)	CHEST (yd / m) 34–36in / 86–91cm	CHEST (yd / m) 38–40in / 97–101cm	CHEST (yd / m) 42–44in / 107–112cm	CHEST (yd / m) 46–48in / 117–122cm	WRAPS PER INCH
8 ply	8–11 / 5–8mm	150–200 / 140–180	16–18 and 24–30	1,310 / 1,200	1,485 / 1,360	1,660 / 1,520	1,835 / 1,680	14–18
10 ply	10–13 / 6–9mm	120–140 / 110–130	13–14 and 20–24	1,200 / 1,100	1,375 / 1,260	1,550 / 1,410	1,725 / 1,580	10–12

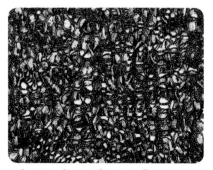

8-ply 100% nylon on 8 / 5mm needles
in stockinette / stocking stitch

BULKY LADDER

Bulky-weight ladder yarns, when knitted firmly, make excellent trims or jewellery. Knitted more openly on larger needles, this yarn can be used to make beautiful accessories. As stitch definition is so poor with ladder yarns, we have included only a stockinette / stocking stitch swatch for this yarn. Knitting a cable or lace stitch with a ladder yarn would not give you a significantly different effect.

GAUGE AND YARDAGE GUIDE

WEIGHT	RECOMMENDED NEEDLE SIZE	YARDAGE PER 100g (yd / m)	GAUGE / TENSION (stitches and rows per 4in / 10cm)	CHEST (yd / m) 34–36in / 86–91cm	CHEST (yd / m) 38–40in / 97–101cm	CHEST (yd / m) 42–44in / 107–112cm	CHEST (yd / m) 46–48in / 117–122cm	WRAPS PER INCH
12 ply	11 / 8mm	50–110 / 45–100	8–12 and 12–18	1,120 / 1,020	1,295 / 1,180	1,470 / 1,340	1,645 / 1,500	6–8

12-ply 90% acrylic, 10% polyester on 15 / 12mm needles in stockinette / stocking stitch

QUICK TIPS

Ladder yarns create an interesting textural effect with an overall lacy look that drapes wonderfully. They are sometimes called train-track yarns.

Ladder yarns are generally not available in Fine weights. Even when they have the appearance of a Fine weight as a yarn, they will knit up to give a Medium-weight appearance due to the three-dimensional character of the tape and fibre tufts.

RARE AND CURIOUS FIBRES

Handknitting yarns include a variety of rare and curious fibres. They are rare because they are new or exotic, or produced in small supply, but they are unusual, luxurious and often beautiful.

VICUNA

The vicuna is a relative of the llama. The tiny scales of its hollow fibres have remarkable insulating and moisture-absorption properties, making it finer, softer, lighter and warmer than any other fibre. It is also the rarest and most expensive, as one animal produces only 1lb (0.45kg) of fibre a year. Vicuna fibre production is strictly controlled and the animals are shorn only twice a year. The short fibres are spun into Lace-weight yarns of 1 ply or 2 ply. The yarn is only available in its natural golden cinnamon colour. It is known by the Incas as the 'yarn of the gods'.

QIVIUT

Qiviut is derived from the fleece of the Arctic musk ox, which sheds its coat naturally. The fibres—remarkably fine, soft, luxurious, warm, and light—are collected when the animals are combed off in the spring. The yarn is shrinkproof and hypoallergenic, and becomes softer with wearing and washing. It tends to sag as it has no elasticity, but is available blended with wool, which counteracts this. Qiviut absorbs dye very well and has superior breathability. It is usually available in 5-ply to 8-ply weights, or mixed with other natural fibres for more versatile yarns. As a pure blend it is a very expensive yarn. It is wonderful for small accessories.

YAK

Yak is spun from the fleece of the Himalayan yak. It is rare, as each animal only sheds enough fibre for one ball of yarn a year. The fibre is extremely fine, smooth, warm and light. It is available in natural shades of blacks, browns and greys, and also in a variety of dyed shades. Less costly than qiviut, it feels just as luxurious and soft. It is available in 8-ply yarns. A very warm fibre, it is good for jumpers and cardigans.

BISON

Bison fibre is spun from the fleece of the American buffalo. Its long staple fibres are separated from the shorter guard hairs of its naturally shed coat to be spun into yarn. It is soft, fluffy, warm, durable and elastic. It contains no lanolin so does not dye well, but is available in lovely natural brown shades. Bison will easily felt if agitated, but does not pill. It is commonly available in 10-ply weights. It absorbs a high level of moisture without feeling wet, so it makes a good choice for warm jumpers, cardigans, jackets and socks.

POSSUM

Possum fibre comes from the brushtail possum. Protected in their native Australia, possum-wool production has offered a solution to the damage the animal causes in New Zealand by killing it for its fur. The fluffy and hollow short-hair fibre is warm, insulating, and light. It is often mixed with wool to provide a durable yarn blend in weights from 3 ply to 8 ply. A good choice for warm winter garments and accessories.

CORN

Corn fibre is extracted from the dextrose of the corncob. Highly processed, it is regarded as a natural plastic. It has all the comfort characteristics of natural fibres such as cotton, silk, and wool, and all the performance, economy, and easy-care nature of synthetic fibres. It has excellent resiliency, great crimp retention, good moisture-wicking properties, a silky feel and good drape. It is available in Medium-weight yarns from 5 ply to 8 ply. A great choice for children's knits.

MILK PROTEIN

Through a bioengineering process, milk-protein fibres are dewatered and wet-spun into a durable yarn that resembles silk in its glossy and luxurious appearance and its soft, light feel. The fibre is antibacterial, antifungal, easy to dye and light-fast. Milk fibre blends well with other fibres and is available in a range of Medium-weight yarns from 3 ply to 5 ply. Its good moisture absorbance makes it cool to wear in summer. Good for lightweight accessories and garments.

NETTLE

Bark from the nettle plant is stripped, soaked and separated into fibres for spinning. Nettle fibre has a long, white, fibrous appearance and is soft and cool to the touch, similar to linen and hemp. It has a hollow core that wicks moisture from the body, keeping the skin cool in summer and warm in winter. Nettle fibre is popular as a handspun yarn. It is available in Fine- and Medium-weight yarns from 4 ply to 8 ply. Usually available in its natural colour, which has a lovely rustic finish and light slub, it will soften with wear. Perfect for summery cardigans or homewares. Nettle is a sustainable fibre, as it grows wild without the use of pesticides or fertilisers.

KENAF

Derived from the bark and core of *Hibiscus cannabinus* L, kenaf is similar to jute, with its slightly coarse and inelastic nature, but much softer. It is often mixed with cotton, which creates a more sustainable yarn blend, as kenaf is more environmentally friendly than cotton. Available as a Fine-weight yarn in 3 ply or 4 ply, it is three-dimensional knitted, which creates an interesting textural look for bags or cushions.

SEACELL

Seacell is a cellulose fibre derived from seaweed. It is smooth, light and shiny, with high tensile strength. It is moisture-absorbent and breathes well, and is temperature-regulating, so keeps the body cool in summer and warm in winter. Seacell is commonly mixed with other fibres and is available as a Fine-weight yarn in 3 ply to 5 ply and as a Medium-weight 8-ply yarn. A popular new craft fibre, it is available in many handspun varieties. It is ideal for knitting shawls, wraps, scarves and lightweight garments.

CALCULATING YARN SUBSTITUTES

There are several reasons why you may want to substitute a yarn. Below are some general guidelines to assist you in this.

REASONS YOU MIGHT NEED OR WANT TO SUBSTITUTE YARN:

- The suggested yarn is too expensive for your budget, or you want to test a pattern with a cheaper yarn choice before you knit with the real thing.

- You don't like the colour choices in the suggested yarn range and would prefer another.

- You are allergic or sensitive to a suggested yarn, and would prefer a more non-allergenic yarn choice.

- The suggested yarn may not be readily available or has been discontinued. Yarn substitute knowledge is especially handy if you are working from a vintage knitting pattern.

- You would like to use a different yarn weight to what is suggested in the knitting pattern, to make it more suitable for your climate or personal preference. You might have a favourite winter jumper pattern that you'd like to reknit in a summer or trans-seasonal yarn.

- You may prefer a different feel and surface texture to the suggested yarn.

- You may have chosen the yarn first because you fell in love with it, and are looking for a suitable knitting pattern for it.

GAUGE

The most important aspect to yarn substitution is yarn gauge. Refer to the suggested yarn gauge for the knitted test swatch dimensions. This information will tell you how many stitches and rows you require to make a 4in (10cm) square. Your substitute yarn will need to be a close match to the number of stitches and rows needed for 4in (10cm). Wash your test swatch and give it a light press, as there are many yarns that change in size after washing.

WRAPS PER INCH

Wraps per inch (wpi) is a handy method, familiar to weavers and handspinners, for quickly measuring a yarn's gauge. Use a ruler to wrap the yarn thread around and count the threads over the distance of one inch. From this count you can determine the gauge of your yarn and what needle size will work best with it. I have included wpi information in the gauge and yardage guide charts under every fibre entry in this book; refer to these to determine the yarn weight for the yarn you are testing.

DRAPE AND ELASTICITY

Drape and elasticity are crucial elements to consider when substituting yarn. If you would like to match the look of the knitted item in your knitting pattern, stick closely to the drape and elasticity specifications of the suggested yarn. For example, if you substitute cotton for wool the finished garment may drop and sag excessively because cotton is less elastic than wool; conversely, using wool instead of cotton may shrink or distort the fit of the finished garment.

FIBRE CONTENT

Fibre content will affect the performance and overall look of the knitted pattern. Look at the information supplied on the yarn character to judge its suitability as a substitute yarn. For example, acrylic mixed with nylon is a good substitute for wool, as the nylon adds enough elasticity to match that of wool.

YARN SPIN

The yarn spin will affect the physical and mechanical properties of a yarn. Study the spin of the suggested yarn closely to find a suitable substitute match. Look out for the following characteristics:

- Single-ply roving or many threads plied together
- Number of threads in the ply
- Loose or tight spin
- Even or uneven spin
- Worsted spin—long staple fibres running in the same direction for a smooth yarn; or woollen spin—short fibres with a more bumpy yarn spin, but light and aerated; for example, tweed

STITCH DEFINITION

Judge the knitting pattern yarn requirements by the knitted stitch and its surface texture. If it includes fancy stitches, choose a yarn with good stitch definition that has a smooth surface, as a fluffly or textured yarn will not show up the stitches as effectively. If the knitting pattern uses a textured yarn for effect then use something similar.

YARDAGE

Calculate the yardage for a substitute yarn by checking the total yarn requirements of the item you wish to knit. For example, if the suggested requirement for the pattern is 10 x 50g balls, each with a yardage of 92yd, the total yardage is 9,200. If the substitute yarn offers 110yd per 50g ball, divide the total yardage by the yardage of a single ball to obtain the number of balls required overall:

9,200yd divided by 110yd = 8.3 balls

Of course, you always need to round up, so in this example you would need to buy 9 balls.

CARE INSTRUCTIONS AND WEARABILITY

The care instructions of a yarn will affect the end result of the knitted garment in terms of its drape, softness, shrinkage, and performance. Many fibres change with wearing and washing; some soften and increase their drape more, some pill, and some shrink. If any of these factors are the reason why you want to substitute the suggested yarn, refer to the specific yarn information for consideration.

YARN LABELS

It is important to understand the information provided on yarn labels and to be able to decode the symbols on them. There is no standardised label system, and information can vary considerably between yarn manufacturers. However, most labels provide the general information listed below.

YARN WEIGHT

A yarn weight is usually suggested to provide information on the use of a yarn. A ply is a number ranging from the finest to the heaviest yarn weights (usually between 1 ply and 14 ply). Alternatively, a name of weight may be given, such as 'lace' for very fine yarns; 'DK' for Medium-weight yarns, and 'bulky' for heavier yarns.

There is also a system, used mostly in the US, of numbering yarn weights from 0 to 5, where 0 is the finest yarn and 5 the heaviest. Where a yarn weight is not supplied, and the yarn is a textured or novelty yarn, or a thick-and-thin yarn, it can usually be knitted in a range of gauges.

GAUGE AND NEEDLE SIZE

Yarn gauge is specified by the number of stitches and rows in a 4in (10cm) square, generally knitted in stocking stitch, and using a specific needle size. Sometimes the yarn label supplies the measurement of 1in (2.5cm), but it is worthwhile knitting a bigger square to get a better understanding of the yarn's drape and performance. If the label does not specify a gauge, or says 'various', the yarn is usually a novelty one that can be knitted with smaller needles to achieve a firmer texture, or larger needles for a lacier texture.

FIBRE CONTENT

A yarn's fibre content is usually supplied on the label, for example: 80% bamboo, 20% wool.

YARDAGE AND WEIGHT

The label will tell you the total length of yarn in a ball or skein. This will help you work out how much you will need for a certain knitting project; whether the yarn is good value for money, and suggests the yarn weight (whether it is Fine, Medium, or Bulky).

COLOUR NUMBER AND DYE LOT

Dye lots are important if you require multiple balls of yarn of the same colour for your knitting project. Always buy yarn from the same dye lot, as dye lots do vary in colour, and even a subtle variation may show up in the final piece.

CARE INSTRUCTIONS

Care instructions provide vital information on how to wash and dry a knitted garment. The main care symbols are listed in the table opposite.

Recommended tension or gauge on the needle size

The gauge swatch will show the number of rows and stitches that should make a 4 x 4in (10 x 10cm) swatch, sometimes abbreviated as **M** for measure, **St** for stitches, or **R** for rows.

Indicates the recommended needle size for making solid fabric

The needle size is sometimes indicated only with a number

Sometimes both US and UK sizes are supplied

This is only a recommended size, and you can adjust the needle size according to your tension. If you have a firm knitting tension you can go up a needle size; if your tension is on the looser side, go down a size

CARE INSTRUCTIONS

Handwash in lukewarm water

Handwash in warm water

Do not machine- or handwash

Three variations of the machine-washable symbols. A delicate cycle is advisable for all handknitted items; set the machine cycle to match the wash temperature

DRYING INSTRUCTIONS

Lay flat to dry

Sometimes this symbol appears under the washing symbols

Machine dryable

If a temperature is indicated, follow that recommendation

Do not machine dry

IRONING INSTRUCTIONS

Press with a cool iron

Press with a warm iron

Press with a hot iron

Do not iron

BLEACHING

Chlorine bleaching okay

Always test bleach on a sample swatch of the yarn

Do not use bleach

DRYING-CLEANING INSTRUCTIONS

Do not dry-clean

Can be dry-cleaned with all solutions

Can be dry-cleaned only with fluorocarbon or petroleum-based solutions

Can be dry-cleaned only with perchlorethylene, fluorocarbon, or petroleum-based solutions

NEEDLE SIZES

Needle sizes generally range from 2mm to 25mm. Most needles are now sold in metric sizes globally. However, American manufacturers still use a system specific to the USA, in which the smaller the needle size, the smaller the number.

Historically, the UK also had its own system of needle sizing, although the metric system has largely replaced this. We include UK needle sizes here for reference in case you are using a vintage knitting pattern and need to convert, or have found some vintage knitting needles, for example in a charity or secondhand shop. In this UK system, the smaller the needle size, the bigger the number.

USA	METRIC	UK
0	2mm	14
1	2.25mm	13
-	2.5mm	-
2	2.75mm	12
-	3mm	11
3	3.25mm	10
4	3.5mm	-
5	3.75mm	9
6	4mm	8
7	4.5mm	7
8	5mm	6
9	5.5mm	5
10	6mm	4
10½	6.5mm	3
-	7mm	2
-	7.5mm	1
11	8mm	0
13	9mm	00
15	10mm	000
17	12.5mm	-
19	15.5mm	-
35	19mm	-
50	25mm	-

US / EUROPEAN GLOSSARY

American and European knitting terms and measurements sometimes differ; this can be confusing when following instructions or yarn requirements from a knitting pattern or reading information from a yarn label. The following tables will assist in converting information.

CONVERSION FORMULAS

To convert inches to centimetres, multiply by 2.54; to convert centimetres to inches, multiply by 0.394
To convert yards to metres, multiply by 0.914; to convert metres to yards, multiply by 1.094
To convert ounces to grams, multiply by 28.35; to convert grams to ounces, multiply by 0.035

KNITTING TERMS

US	UK
Gauge	Tension
Bind on	Cast on
Bind off	Cast off
Stockinette stitch	Stocking stitch
Seed stitch	Moss stitch
Plain knitting/ garter stitch	Garter stitch
Skein	Hank
Yarn over	Yarn round needle/ forward

MEASUREMENT CONVERSIONS

IMPERIAL	METRIC
$\frac{1}{8}$in	3mm
$\frac{3}{8}$in	1cm
1in	2.54cm
12in (1ft)	30cm
1yd	91.44cm
1yd 3in	1m

WEIGHT CONVERSIONS

IMPERIAL	METRIC
1oz	28g
1lb (16oz)	450g
2lb 3oz	1kg (1,000g)

GENERAL GLOSSARY

abrasion-resistance: the ability of a fibre, yarn or knitted structure to be scratch- or itch-free against the skin.

antifungal: the ability of a yarn or fibre to resist attacks from moulds and mildews, which makes it antibacterial, as these are the substances that can cause and accelerate the growth of bacteria in fibres.

aran:
knitting technique: a traditional knitting technique from Ireland and Scotland.
yarn: a natural lanolin-coated raw yarn, usually handspun.
yarn weight: (capitalised) a medium weight.

artisan: handspun or hand-tailored yarns, usually made in limited editions, small productions or one-off batches.

bast: refers to vegetable fibres made from the tissue of the plant.

belly band: the packaging band or label on balls or skeins that gives information about the yarn.

bias: a knitting structure that leans diagonally, whether occurring from the yarn spin or the knitted stitch pattern.

bind off: the knitting of stitches to close or end knitting securely.

biodegradable: capable of decomposing naturally without the harmful environmental damage of disposing of waste and garbage.

bleed: dye washing off a yarn or knitted fabric, where the dye is visible in the wash water.

bobbles: a knitting technique that makes raised bobbles on the knit surface. Sometimes referred to as blackberry stitch.

bouclé: a yarn-spinning method of plying two or more threads together; one thread is spun more loosely than the other, which causes a curl or loop to form over the base thread.

breathability: the ability of a knitted structure or yarn to circulate air for a comfortable body temperature.

brushed: knitted fabric or yarn with the surface texture of a very light fur coating.

bulky:
knitting weight: a heavy, thick, or warm knitted structure in a fabric; also referred to as 'chunky'.
yarn weight: (capitalised) a heavy yarn weight, or a thick yarn.

buoyancy: elasticity, airiness and lightness of weight in a yarn.

cable: a textured knitting technique of crossing vertical rib sequences.

cast off: the knitting of stitches to close or end knitting securely. Also referred to as bind off.

cast on: the creating of stitches on a knitting needle to begin knitting.

chenille: a textured yarn with tufted pile on a base thread.

chunky:
knitting weight: a heavy or thick knitted structure in a fabric. Also referred to as 'bulky'.
yarn weight: a heavy or thick yarn.

cobweb:
knitting: a delicate and wispy lacy appearance.
yarn: the finest or smallest yarn weight; also referred to as a Super Fine or Lace yarn or 1-ply yarn weight.

cohesion: the ability of fibres to hold together in a yarn spin, creating a reliable structure.

colour-fastness: the ability of a yarn or knitted structure to maintain its original colour without fading.

colour retention: the ability of a yarn or knitted structure to absorb dye and reflect colour.

colourwork: a knitting technique using two or more colours for jacquard, chevron, and picture knitting.

Craft: a heavy yarn weight, or a thick yarn.

crimp: a natural wave or curl in a fibre, which creates a springiness or elasticity. It also causes matting or felting of fibres.

darning: the sewing of seam edges in a knitted item.

de-ball: when a ball of yarn loosens from its ball structure and tangles easily.

dehairing: a fibre production process where short guard-hair fibres are separated from the longer, finer fibres before spinning. The long, fine fibres produce better-quality yarn.

DK (double knitting): the finest of the Medium-weight yarn categories, and the most popular knitting yarn weight. Also referred to as Light Worsted.

drape: drape is the ease and flow of movement in a garment. The softer the flow of a knitted fabric, the more drape it has; the sturdier the fabric, the less drape it has.

durability: the long-lasting performance of a knitted fabric.

dye retention: the ability of a fibre or yarn to absorb coloration and maintain it during washing without colour-bleed.

elasticity: the flexibility of a knitted stitch and how effectively it holds its shape. Springier, crimped yarns have greater elasticity than smooth or stiff fibres.

eyelash: a yarn type that has tufts and threads attached to a core yarn.

felting: the matting of a fibre or knitted fabric that produces a firm structure. This is a natural process of some fibres caused by the movement of their microscopic scales when exposed to excess heat and friction.

fibre: a natural or synthetic filament that may be spun into a yarn.

fibre-shedding: the shedding of fibre and fluff from the core of a yarn or knitted structure.

fibrous: the appearance of a yarn or knitted structure that is sinewy or stringy.

Fingering: a Fine-yarn weight measurement equivalent to a 4-ply yarn weight.

fire retardancy: the ability of a fabric or knitted structure to reduce flammability or combustion.

flamme: a loosely plied thick-and-thin yarn.

fuzzy: a yarn or knitted structure that has a furry or fluffy texture.

gauge: the specified number of stitches and rows per inch of knitting, with a certain needle size, to determine a yarn weight required for a knitting pattern.

guard hairs: the coarser hairs of animal fleece, which are usually separated from the finer hairs before spinning.

heathered: a yarn that is spun using a blend of pre-coloured fibres, whether natural or dyed, so the yarn appearance is slightly mottled.

honeycomb: a knitting technique that gives a repetitive surface pattern that creates hollows between the surface pattern and base fabric.

hypoallergenic yarn: yarn designed to reduce or minimise the possibility of an allergic response, as the material contains relatively few or no potentially irritating substances.

insulative: the ability of a yarn or knitted structure to hold in warmth in cold weather, and retain coolness in warm weather.

jacquard: a knitting technique using two or more colours following patterned graphs to create a knitted pattern.

lace:
fabric: an open, airy, delicate fabric construction.
stitch: a decorative knitted stitch created from making holes and twists in a repeated pattern while knitting.
yarn weight: (capitalised) a Fine-yarn weight measurement equivalent to a 2-ply yarn.

lanolin: a naturally occurring wax found in some animal fleece that is waterproofing and insulating.

Light Fingering: a Fine-yarn weight measurement equivalent to a 3-ply yarn.

Light Worsted: the finest of the Medium-weight yarn categories. Also referred to as DK.

loft: the lightness of a yarn, referring to how much air it holds or is trapped in its fibre.

lustre: the surface radiance of a yarn or knitted structure.

memory: a yarn or knitted fabric's ability to return to its original form.

mesh: a ribbon or tape yarn that has an open knitted or woven interlocking structure.

metallic: a yarn or knitted structure that has the lustre of metal.

moiré: a fibre or yarn with a silky, wavy appearance.

moisture resistance: the ability of a yarn or knitted structure to resist moisture on its surface and not absorb it.

moisture wicking: see wicking.

mottled: a yarn that has a spotted or blotchy appearance.

nap: the fuzzy, downy coating of the surface of a knitted fabric or yarn.

needle size: the size of the knitting needles required to knit a certain yarn weight.

noil: the short fibre left after combing wool or spinning silk; these fibres are often used to add character to yarns such as rovings.

novelty yarn: a non-conventional yarn spin that is fancy or fashionable for the moment.

nubbly: the textured bumpy surface appearance of a knitted fabric or yarn.

open-lace: a knitting stitch creating a fabric with large holes in a repeated pattern. This is usually achieved with needles that are larger than recommended for the yarn. Sometimes referred to as open-weave.

organic: fibres that are produced without the use of chemicals in farming, growing, harvesting and production.

over-drape: the tendency of a garment to sag or drop due to its own weight.

pilling: the excess gathering of fluff on a knitted fabric or yarn, caused by the separation of the short fibres from the long.

ply: the twisting together of two or more strands.

Polar: a thick yarn that is also referred to as polar fleece, which describes a synthetic fleece texture.

resilience: the ability of a knitted structure to maintain its original form.

ripple:
knitting: a knitting technique that makes wavy zigzag lines. Can be three-dimensional with raised stitches, and can be colourwork.
yarn: the character of the yarn, having an undulating or wavy look.

roving: a long, narrow strip of fibre prepared for spinning. Can also refer to a single-ply yarn that is loosely twisted and felted as a thick yarn (capitalised).

Rug: a heavy yarn weight, or a thick yarn.

shrinkage: the calculated decreasing of size of a knitted stitch or fabric post-knitting and post-washing.

skein: a length of yarn wound into a long coil as opposed to a ball.

slippage: the unwanted slipping of stitches off a needle while knitting.

slub: the fibre bump found in an uneven yarn spin.

snags: knitted stitches that are pulled or caught accidently from the knitted structure, causing large unsightly loops.

spongy: a yarn or knitted structure that has a light, porous and elastic appearance or feel.

staple fibres: the cluster of fibres from animal fleece held together by cross fibres. Also refers to fibres from all sources (vegetable, animal, synthetic) that are prepared for spinning.

static: a fibre, yarn or knitted structure that creates an electrical crackle, which is caused by movement and friction.

sticky: yarns that tend to matt or stick together during knitting.

stitch definition: the clarity or visibility of a knitted stitch.

Super Bulky: the heaviest or thickest of the yarn weights.

Super Fine: the finest or lightest yarn weight; this resembles a 1-ply or 2-ply yarn.

surface texture: the visual and tactile quality of a knitted fabric.

sustainable: capable of being produced steadily without exhausting natural resources and causing severe ecological damage.

tape: a ribbon yarn type that is knitted or woven as a flat tape.

tensile strength: refers to the stress a yarn or textile can endure while being stretched, without weakening or breaking.

tension: the firmness or looseness with which one knits.

textured effects:
    knitting: a technique that creates a three-dimensional appearance, such as cable or honeycomb.
    yarn: a yarn that is designed and manufactured as a three-dimensional form to create a textured look when knitted; for example, bouclé, ribbon and eyelash yarns.

thermo-regulating: the ability of a yarn or knitted structure to keep one cool in warm weather and warm in cold weather.

three-dimensional: the appearance of a knitted structure that has depth and height rather than flatness.

trans-seasonal: an in-between season yarn or knitted fabric that is neither too warm nor too cool, but can provide suitable coverage for light weather wear. Also referred to as inter-seasonal.

tube: a ribbon yarn type that is knitted or woven in a hollow tube formation.

tweed:
    twist: a traditional yarn-twisting process using short, uneven and recycled fibres.
    yarn: a slubby, textured wool yarn.

twist:
    knitting: a knitting technique that crosses over one or more stitches.
    yarn: 1) the direction in which the yarn is spun; 2) variables of tension of a yarn; for example, loose twist; 3) the unwanted writhing or squirming of a yarn while knitting.

variegated: a yarn with various colours in it.

wicking: the ability of a knitted structure or yarn to absorb moisture (perspiration) off and away from the skin.

worming: when a yarn detaches from the knitting and coils back on itself.

worsted:
    spinning: a spinning process where long fibres run parallel for a smooth continuous spinning.
    yarn weight: (capitalised) a mid- to heavy yarn weight.

wraps per inch (wpi): a method of measuring a yarn gauge by wrapping the yarn thread around the distance of an inch. The number of threads covering the inch is the total wpi. The more threads over the inch, the finer the yarn gauge; the fewer threads, the heavier the yarn gauge.

wrinkle-resistance: the ability of a yarn or knitted structure to uncrease after being creased or folded.

yardage: the number of yards or metres in a ball or skein of yarn. It is used to help determine how much yarn one requires for a knitted item, or the weight of a yarn.

yarn spin: the method used for spinning yarn.

yarn swift: a tool used to hold a yarn skein while winding off.

RESOURCES

KNITTING TIPS

There are a vast number of online forums that supply knitting tips, helpful hints and knitting patterns, from independent knitters to chat forums and yarn companies. It is not possible to supply an exhaustive list, so I chose the following based on clarity of information and a good choice of knitting techniques.

DAILYKNITTER.COM
A lovely-looking website with patterns, knitting help, book and yarn reviews, and a directory of knitting sites and forums.

PATONSYARNS.COM.AU
A website with an illustrated guide to knitting techniques. Also supplies free downloadable knitting patterns.

LANAGROSSA.COM
Offers free downloadable knitting tips and techniques, including specialist techniques such as 'binding off Italian style' and 'fringing'.

KNITTING ASSOCIATIONS

CRAFTYARNCOUNCIL.COM
A knitting association website representing yarn companies, accessory manufacturers, magazine and book publishers, and consultants in the yarn industry. This is a valuable resource for knitters of all levels. It supplies a calendar of knitting events and expos and links to guilds and groups.

TKGA.COM
The knitting guild association is a membership guild website with links to books, magazines, groups and events.

YARN SUPPLY AND YARN INFORMATION

There is a daunting choice of online knitting-supply stores. However, there are very few stores that present information beautifully with easy-to-read websites, and that also have good, reliable customer service. I list a few recommended sites below.

JOSHARP.COM
A beautifully designed website from a manufacturer that supplies its own range of yarn and patterns. It also provides information on the welfare of the sheep from which it sources its yarns.

YARNMARKET.COM
An online store supplying a wide range of yarns sourced from around the globe. Allows you to search by yarn weight, fibre type and yarn brand. Also has a category on eco-friendly fibres. Provides good descriptions of each yarn with suggested knitting uses.

KNITPICKS.COM
An online yarn supplier with a diverse range of yarns sourced globally, as well as knitting kits, tools and patterns. This site also has tutorials for all knitting levels and links to online knitting community forums.

INDEX

YARN WEIGHTS

There is no standardised measurement system of yarn weights, and there is much variety between yarn manufacturers' references to weights. There is a general guide and reference system, however, which this yarn weight conversion chart can assist with.

STANDARDISED YARN WEIGHT	US	UK / EUROPE	AUSTRALIA / NZ
0 LACE	Thread Cobweb Lace Light Fingering	1 ply 2 ply 3 ply	1 ply 2 ply 3 ply
1 SUPER FINE	Fingering Baby	Sock 4 ply	4 ply
2 FINE	Sport	Light DK 5 ply	5 ply
3 LIGHT	DK Light Worsted	DK 8 ply	8 ply
4 MEDIUM	Worsted Fisherman Aran	Aran 10 ply	10 ply
5 BULKY	Bulky Rug Craft	Chunky	12 ply
6 SUPER BULKY	Super Bulky Roving Polar	Super Chunky Polar	14 ply